UNIX® Survival Guide

UNIX® Survival Guide

Tim Parker

Addison-Wesley Publishing Company, Inc.
Reading, Massachusetts   Menlo Park, California   New York
Don Mills, Ontario   Wokingham, England   Amsterdam   Bonn   Sydney
Singapore   Tokyo   Madrid   San Juan

Many of the designations used by manufacturers and sellers to distinguish their products are claimed as trademarks. Where those designations appear in this book and Addison-Wesley was aware of a trademark claim, the designations have been printed in initial capital letters.

Library of Congress Cataloging-in-Publication Data

Parker, Tim, 1958-
    UNIX survival guide / Tim Parker.
       p.   cm.
    Includes index.
    ISBN 0-201-57078-5
    1. UNIX (Computer operating system)   I. Title.
QA76.76.063P365   1990
005.4'3--dc20   90-45507
                                               CIP

Copyright © 1990 by Tim Parker

All rights reserved. No part of this publication may be reproduced, stored in a retrieval system, or transmitted, in any form or by any means, electronic, mechanical, photocopying, recording, or otherwise, without the prior written permission of the publisher. Printed in the United States of America. Published simultaneously in Canada.

Managing Editor: Amorette Pedersen
Copy Editor: Kate Johnson
Set in 11-point Palatino by Benchmark Productions

ABCDEFGHIJ-MW-943210
First Printing, October 1990

This one, of course, is for my parents.

Gratias tibi ago.

Acknowledgments

I have spent the last 10 years quite happily writing about computers for magazines. Writing a book, I had assumed, was just like writing a long magazine article. The truth is, it is quite a bit different.

Seldom is a book the product of one person. There are editors and publishers who take the material the author writes and turn it into a finished product. This book is no exception, and thanks are due. Vince Leone of Sybex Computer Books read through my first drafts and showed me how a book should really be written. Chris Williams and Amy Pedersen of Benchmark Productions took my material and with the work of Kate Johnson as copy editor, produced the product you now hold. These people are responsible for the book: I merely supplied the basic content.

The Santa Cruz Operation (SCO) graciously provided the software I used through this book, including their XENIX and UNIX products, Open Desktop, and several of their applications.

Dell Computer Corporation kindly provided a Dell System 325 in the early months. Acer Corporation made one of their excellent 80386-based systems available for the rest of the writing process.

Thanks are also due to J. D. Hildebrand, then editor of Computer Language Magazine, who now edits UNIX Review. He was instrumental in my beginning to think about turning rough chapters into a book. Also, thanks are due to UNIX Review's columnist Stan Kelly-Bootle, who helped speed the original idea along.

Finally, those who supported my efforts deserve a grateful nod. My parents provided the encouragement, and occasionally helped out the perpetually impecunious author. My detours from matters at hand were tolerated by Bill Lenardon of MultiCAP Inc, who markets the CARES system for real estate offices that started all of this. My friends (who know who they are) provided support and occasional diversions. Lastly, thanks to Ingrid, who provides all my soul needs.

Table of Contents

Preface   xvii

Chapter 1
An Introduction to UNIX   1

  What are Operating Systems?   2
  UNIX   5
      UNIX Moves to Micros   6
      The Parts of UNIX   7
      The Advantages of UNIX   7

Chapter 2
Getting Started   11

  Accessing UNIX   11
      Logging In   12
      Logging Out   15
      Identifying Your Terminal   16
  Beginning to Use UNIX   18
      The Shell   18
      Is Anyone Out There? (The who Command)   19

Changing Your Password (The passwd Command)	20
Testing, Testing...	22
Summary	23

Chapter 3
Managing Files and Directories Efficiently — 25

Using Files	25
Getting a List of Your Files (The l Command)	26
Displaying Your Files (The cat and more Commands)	30
Deleting Your Files (The rm Command)	33
Renaming Your Files (The mv Command)	35
Copying Your Files (The cp Command)	35
File Permissions	36
Redirection and Piping	37
Organizing Your Work with Directories	39
The Directory Structure	39
Users' Home Directories (The pwd Command)	40
Moving About Directories (The cd Command)	42
Creating Directories Yourself (The mkdir Command)	43
Removing Your Directories (The rmdir Command)	45
Copying and Renaming Directories (The copy Command)	46
Summary	47

Chapter 4
Using Printers and Background Processing — 49

Using a Printer	50
Sending a File to a Printer (The lp and pr Commands)	50
Sending to a Printer Using Redirection	52
Getting Printer Status Information	52
Cancelling a Print Request (The cancel Command)	54
Controlling Processes	55
Delaying the Start of a Process (The at Command)	55
Using Background Processing to Do Several Tasks at Once	56

Killing a Process (The ps and kill Commands)	57
Summary	58

Chapter 5
The Mail Program — 61

Different Versions	61
Your Mailbox	62
Using Mail: A Quick Example	63
Sending Mail	65
Reading Mail	65
Saving Your Mail (The mb and s Commands)	67
Deleting, Undeleting, Replying, and Forwarding Mail	68
Deleting and Undeleting	68
Replying to a Mail Message	69
Forwarding a Mail Message	69
Saving Time with Mailing Lists (The alias Command)	70
The .mailrc File	71
Summary	71

Chapter 6
Using the Editors ed and vi — 73

A Little About Editors	73
Using ed	74
Entering Text with ed (The a, p, w, and q Commands)	75
Reading in an Existing File (The e and r Commands)	76
Getting to Know ed	77
Deleting, Inserting, Changing, and Moving Lines	79
Searching for Text (The / and ? Commands)	80
Replacing Text (The s, g, v, and u Commands)	82
The vi Editor	85
Creating and Exiting a File	85
Moving Around the Screen	87

Simple Editing with vi ... 87
Searching and Replacing Text ... 90
Copying and Moving Lines ... 92
Summary ... 94

Chapter 7
Completing the Fundamentals ... 97

Finding a File (The find Comment) ... 97
Linking Files Together (The ln Command) ... 99
More Ways to List Files (The ls Command) ... 101
Printing the Listing Commands ... 102
Comparing Files (The cmp and diff Commands) ... 103
Counting Lines, Words, or Characters (The wc Command) ... 106
Sorting a File (The sort Command) ... 106
Searching for Patterns (The grep Commands) ... 109
Using the UNIX Calendar (The cal Command) ... 111
Creating Date-Based Reminders ... 112

Chapter 8
The Shell ... 115

What Is a Shell? ... 115
The UNIX Shells ... 116
The PATH ... 117
Wildcards ... 119
Pipes and Redirection ... 120
Metacharacters ... 122
Creating a Shell Program ... 123
The Bourne, C, and Korn Shells ... 124

Chapter 9
Getting to Know the Shell ... 127

Shell Variables	128
Variable Types and Assignments	129
The .profile File	135
Shell Program Flow	136
The test Command	137
The if Statement	138
The case Statement	142
while and for Loops	144
Breaking a Loop	146
Getting Proficient with Shell Programming	147

Chapter 10
Basic System Administration   *149*

The Superuser Account	150
Starting and Stopping the UNIX System	151
Starting the System	151
Choosing the Operating Mode	152
Shutting Down the System	153
Moving to System Maintenance Mode Without Rebooting	154
Maintaining File Systems	155
How to Keep Space Free	155
Checking the Free Space	157
Maintaining User Accounts	158
User Groups	159
Adding a User	160
Removing a User	162
Changing a User	163
Using .profile or .login	164
Copying Files with copy and cp	166
Automating Processes with cron and at	167
Processor Status	170

Chapter 11
Providing for Security   175

   Physical Security   175
   Access Security   176
   Changing User Passwords   177
      File Permissions In Detail   179
   The File Creation Mask and umask   180
   Changing File Permissions with chmod   181
      Changing Owners and Groups   184
   Backups   185
   Sources of Damage   185
   Backup Media   187
   The Backup Schedule   188
      The Backup Log   190
      The backup Account   191
   Using tar for Backups   192
   Process Accounting   195
   Starting and Stopping Process Accounting   195
   Accessing Process Accounting Information   196

Chapter 12
Peripherals and Devices   199

   Device Files and Numbers   199
   How UNIX Uses a Terminal   201
      The "gettydefs" File   203
      Adding a Terminal   204
      Troubleshooting   206
      Adding a Modem   207
   Printers   207
      Connecting a Printer   208
      The Print Spooler   209
   Controlling the Spooler   211

Chapter 13
UNIX Standards and GUIs — 215

- Defining a Standard UNIX — 215
- GUIs — 216
    - A Brief GUI History — 218
    - X Windows — 220
- The Evolution of UNIX — 222

Appendix A
UNIX Commands and Options — 225

Appendix B
Alphabetical Listing of Commands — 235

Index — 245

Preface

This book originally started as a short manual for system administrators, to accompany a large UNIX software program I had written for the real estate market. Even though that software prevented a user from ever seeing UNIX, one or two people in an office still had to manage the system, and deal with UNIX head on every day. The system administration material was useful, but I had assumed a basic familiarity with UNIX, which most of the users did not have.

Although there were several good UNIX books available, none seemed to fit the image of a book I had envisioned for these circumstances, a book which these computer neophytes could work with. I therefore began developing some basic UNIX material to include in my software's documentation. Through the course of the following two years, the documentation refined itself into a complete book.

Originally, this book was intended to be the comprehensive guide to UNIX. However, several months worth of work quickly made it obvious that this could not be achieved while still aiming the material at a newcomer to UNIX.

Chapter 1

An Introduction to UNIX

Just what is UNIX? As you shall see shortly, it is a way of getting a lot of performance out of a computer, without necessarily knowing anything about the machinery. UNIX is also one of the most powerful operating systems available. But don't worry, UNIX is not as complex or difficult to learn as many people think it is. It is different from other computer operating systems, but these differences are what make UNIX so attractive.

Whether or not you have used computers before doesn't really matter. This book will give you a working knowledge of UNIX as painlessly as possible. If you have used a computer, you will probably be able to relate some of the material to your previous experience, but this is by no means necessary. It is easy to learn UNIX: You really have to know only a few commands and these are not difficult to remember.

All UNIX systems have someone who is in charge of the system. This person makes sure that the operating system works properly and consistently, and manages user access to the system. Although the title of this position may differ with each company, it is usually System Administrator or System Manager. If you have any questions about the UNIX system or are experiencing problems, this person should be able to help you.

In this chapter, you will learn just what UNIX is and what it does. If you are eager to get started, you can skip to Chapter 2, but if you would like a little background knowledge, this is the place to get it. If some concepts seem unfamiliar or difficult to grasp right away, don't worry, they will all make sense after you have used (and come to understand) UNIX a little more.

What are Operating Systems?

All modern computers are collections of different pieces of circuit board, silicon chips, and other devices all inter-connected. These pieces are called the computer's *hardware*. All these pieces of hardware together cannot do anything by themselves. Something has to tell the hardware what to do and how to communicate between the parts. The something that does this is software.

Software is a series of instructions for the hardware to perform. These instructions may be about the hardware and how to use it, or they may be instructions about a program that you can use. In some cases, these instructions are "burned" into a silicon chip to tell it how to perform a specific task. This is called *firmware* (to show that it is a combination of hardware and software).

The real "brain" of any computer is a chip called the CPU or *central processing unit*. The CPU allows the computer to add numbers together and send instructions between different parts of the CPU and *memory*. Memory is where the computer stores numbers, letters, and other information when they are not actively being used by the CPU. The CPU makes the computer perform an action by telling other parts of the hardware how to behave. The CPU is told what to tell the rest of the hardware by the software.

The modern computer is a complex electronic marvel; it can accomplish many tasks in very short periods of time. The software that tells it how to do these tasks is similarly complex. In order to make the task of writing software easier, software programs are divided into two major groups. The first group tells the CPU how to control the hardware. The second simply supplies the instructions for accomplishing a given task without worrying about how to make the hardware work.

A set of instructions that together accomplish a specific task are called a *program*. Because they don't need to communicate directly with the hardware, programs in the latter group can be made smaller and are easier to write. This kind of program performs a task of some sort: For example, it calculates numbers in a spreadsheet, displays graphics on the screen, or sorts numbers into ascending order. This type of software is applied by the user to accomplish a task, and is known as *application* software.

Software in the first group—the type of software that talks to the hardware directly—is known as the *operating system*. The operating system acts as a translator between the application software and the hardware. When the application wants to accomplish something with the hardware, the operating system takes over and tells the hardware what to do and then relays the results back to the application when it is finished.

An operating system really "manages" the hardware, and provides the way in which the hardware communicates with users. Sometimes applications take over the communications job, but they all rely on the operating system to control the hardware.

When computers and operating systems were getting started, the hardware was slow, and operating systems had only a few jobs to do. As machines got faster and more additional equipment for the hardware were developed, the operating systems got larger, more complex, and much more important. With today's high-speed microcomputers, operating systems must manage the hardware and all additional equipment in such a manner as not to slow the machinery down. Operating system programming is a long, involved process, and requires a great deal of specialized knowledge.

With the advent of high-speed machines, it became obvious that computers could more than keep up with the requirements of a single person using the system. Indeed, a single person could tell the computer to do many things at once, and it would appear as though the computer were doing so. In actuality, computers can generally only do one thing at a time, but they do things so fast that they can finish one part of a job and then start on another immediately. It appears to the user that both jobs are being worked on at the same time. Each program, command, or instruction from the user to the computer is called a *task*. This capability for handling more than one program "simultaneously" is called *multitasking*.

As hardware continued to speed up with modern electronics, operating systems were redesigned to allow more than one person to use a system at once. This follows the same principle as multitasking in that the hardware is "fooled" into thinking that each user is just one more task. Those systems that permit more than one user at a time are called *multiuser* systems. By their very nature, multiuser systems are always multitasking, but some do not allow each user to do more than one task at a time. Because the term multitasking is usually used to describe a system that allows a user to do several things at once, the latter type of system is not usually described as multitasking.

So, as the hardware improves, so must the operating systems, in order to get the best performance out of the machines. The faster a machine can go, the more tasks (and hence more users) it can support. But designing a multiuser, multitasking operating system is not easy. Many designs have been tried over the years, and most have not worked well. UNIX, one of the more powerful, has evolved into a very efficient operating system, which is accepted industry-wide.

Of course UNIX is not the only multiuser, multitasking operating system. But it is one of the most popular, and for reasons we shall see shortly, it is also one of the best.

UNIX

Bell Telephone Laboratories, the General Electric Company, and Project MAC of the Massachusetts Institute of Technology teamed together in 1965 to develop a new operating system, to be called Multics. Multics was intended to allow simultaneous access to a computer service for many users, and to allow easier sharing of data between them. Although a preliminary version of Multics was written, it did not live up to expectations, so Bell Laboratories ended its involvement.

Several of the Bell Labs people who were involved with the Multics project began to design, on paper, a new file system that would fulfill their needs. Ken Thompson wrote a preliminary version of the *kernel* (the heart of an operating system) for the GE 645 computer, and programs to simulate the new design.

Thompson had also developed a game called "Space Travel", which executed poorly on its target machine (a Honeywell 635). When he encountered an underused PDP-7, Thompson began to investigate moving the game to that machine. Together, Thompson and Dennis Ritchie began to write a working version of their paper system, consisting of the file system, some basic utilities, and a process handler. Another member of their group, Brian Kernighan, named the program UNICS, a pun on Multics. In 1970 the name was changed to UNIX.

The group moved UNIX from a simple system on the PDP-7 to the PDP-11, and began to develop a text-processing environment for the Bell Labs patent department. The early version of UNIX was small, occupying only 16k for the operating system kernel, but gradually grew as new capabilities were added.

In an attempt to develop a FORTRAN compiler on the PDP-11 under UNIX, Thompson ended up developing a language he called B (which was based on another language, called BCPL). B was slow, so Dennis Ritchie refined the language to speed it up, and in the process added several new features.

In 1973, the UNIX system was rewritten in the C language, and the use of UNIX continued to grow inside Bell Labs. For legal reasons, Bell Labs could not market the new system, but they did distribute it to universities that requested copies for educational purposes. Thompson and Ritchie published a paper in the journal *Communications of the ACM* describing UNIX in 1974, and this sparked increased interest in the operating system from universities and business concerns.

As the refinements to the system continued at Bell Labs, and other institutions added their own contributions, many variants of UNIX appeared. In 1982, Bell combined a number of these variants into a single UNIX system called System III. In 1983, more improvements were made, and AT&T finally announced official support for UNIX System V. (System IV was used for internal development but never released as an official version.)

At the same time, the University of California at Berkeley had been modifying their UNIX extensively and released a version called Berkeley Software Distribution UNIX, the latest version of which is UNIX 4.3 BSD.

UNIX Moves to Micros

As microcomputers became more powerful, it seemed that they would also make a good target for UNIX. Microsoft licensed UNIX from AT&T in 1982 and produced a version of UNIX for micros called XENIX. Microsoft later teamed up with a company called the Santa Cruz Operation (SCO) to expand XENIX's capabilities. Since then, Microsoft and SCO have been leading the use of UNIX on microcomputers under the names XENIX and UNIX.

Several versions of UNIX are now available. Each hardware manufacturer that offers a UNIX version has licensed the code, and made some modifications to suit its own environment. Therefore, there are differences between versions, but usually these differences are not noticeable to the end user.

The UNIX industry is currently trying to establish a consistent set of UNIX standards for all versions of the operating system. Whether or not this ever succeeds will depend on corporate politics. This book is based on UNIX System V, as implemented by SCO UNIX 386. Where difference between versions do occur, they are noted.

The Parts of UNIX

UNIX is composed of four basic parts: the kernel, the file system, the shell, and the tools. The four parts all interrelate, as shown in Figure 1.1.

The *kernel* is the nucleus of the operating system. It controls the computer hardware, and translates UNIX commands into hardware commands. The user never has to deal with the kernel directly.

The *file system* is the way UNIX stores information of any kind. Files can contain documents, spreadsheet information, graphic pictures, instructions to UNIX itself, and many other types of data. UNIX treats all files the same and stores them in a file system from which they can easily be retrieved either by the user or by UNIX itself.

The *shell* is a program that acts as the interface between the kernel and the user. As shown in Figure 1.1 on the following page, the kernel is completely "surrounded" by the shell, and all commands given to the shell are passed along to the kernel. The kernel, in turn, translates them to the correct hardware commands.

The *tools* are all programs that can be run by the shell to perform various tasks. When you tell the shell to run a tool, it executes the tool, and lets you interact with the tool directly. Any software that is loaded onto a UNIX system, such as a word processor or database, is technically a tool, although usually, the term "tool" refers to the basic programs supplied with UNIX.

The Advantages of UNIX

UNIX has become popular for many reasons, but a few are especially worth noting. While most of the advantages of using UNIX are primarily aimed at programmers, they do have interesting consequences for the end user as well.

Figure 1.1: The Parts of UNIX

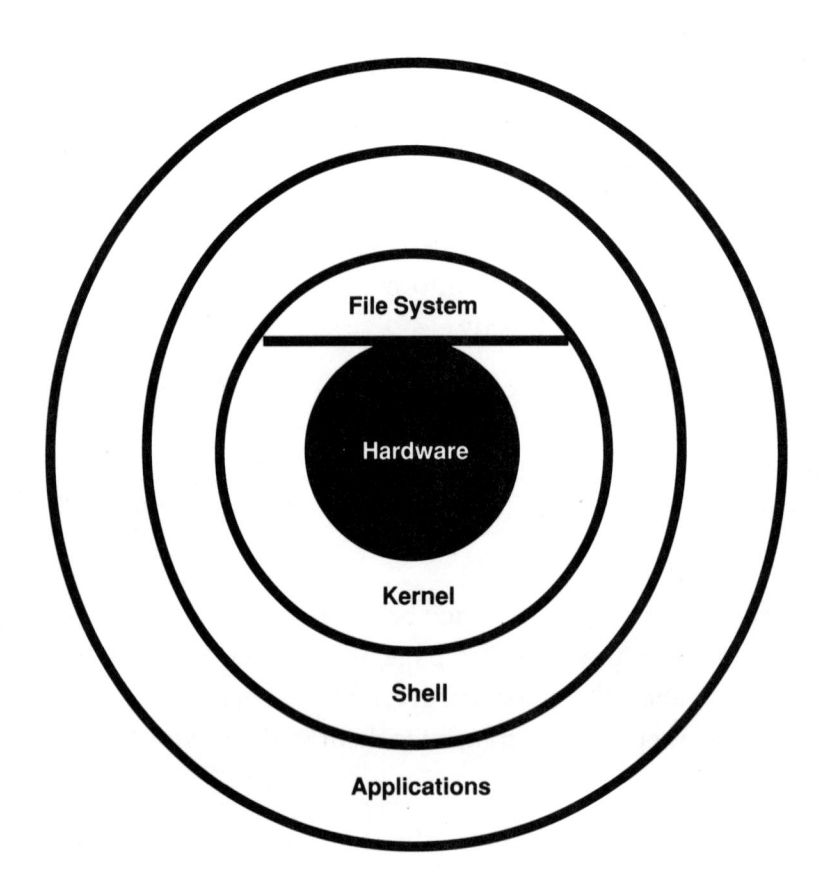

File System

Hardware

Kernel

Shell

Applications

First and foremost, UNIX was written in a high-level language (C), which makes it easy for any competent programmer to understand, modify, and integrate the operating system. As C compiler technology increases, recompilation of the operating system and its utilities produces a corresponding increase in the system's performance. Also, programmers can use the C language to write applications that fit perfectly into the UNIX operating system; a systems programmer need not know one language for applications and another for the operating system.

UNIX is a true multitasking, multiuser system that allows multiple users to each have several tasks executing at once. Further, the UNIX system hides the hardware from the software, so programmers do not have to worry about the specifics of the machines on which their programs will be run.

UNIX employs simple, very powerful user interfaces, which can be readily customized to the user's requirements. The interfaces are also written in C, which enables a programmer to customize a standard commercial interface.

UNIX provides a large number of *primitives*, or basic programs, which can be combined to simplify the task of writing larger and more complex applications. These can then be combined in other ways with other UNIX commands. The shell interfaces themselves provide a simple development language that uses the power of UNIX's utilities to best effect.

The UNIX file system is hierarchical. The file structure is simple and efficient. It permits easy maintenance, and can be used readily by application programs.

Finally, the UNIX method of treating all disk drives, terminals, printers, and other attached peripherals as standard devices allows the use of a consistent interface for all such devices.

All of these advantages add up to a very convenient system for programmers and users. The true power of UNIX is only realized by programming in it, but an end user can appreciate many of these advantages after using the system for a short while.

Chapter 2

Getting Started

In this chapter, you will get right down to the task of using the UNIX system. There is a lot to learn at first, but none of the information is really complicated, and it will all become second nature very quickly.

First, you will learn how to access the UNIX operating system through a terminal. After trying a few simple commands to get a feel for UNIX, you can then use some very powerful UNIX capabilities that few other operating systems offer. Finally, you will examine the UNIX directory structure and learn how you can use directories to your benefit.

After this chapter is finished, you will have actually gotten right into UNIX and performed some complicated procedures, all using very simple commands. You should then be well on your way to becoming a UNIX master!

Accessing UNIX

Terminals provide access to UNIX systems. They come in many different models, from a wide variety of manufacturers. Most are composed of two basic parts: a screen and a keyboard. The most common type of terminal has a full-screen display that can show 24 or 25 lines of text on the screen and 80 columns across. Some terminals offer much more, and others offer less, but "normal" terminals have these dimensions and are referred to as 24x80 or 25x80 terminals.

A terminal can be connected to the UNIX system in one of two ways. Usually, the terminal is connected directly to the UNIX system by a cable attached at the back of the terminal display. This is called a *hard-wired* terminal. Some terminals may be connected to the computer running UNIX via modems. Many of these types of terminals use modems that automatically connect when they are used, but some require the user to dial the UNIX system manually.

There are many other types of terminals, which may lack full screen display, use a printer interface to display activity, or require special operating instructions. If you need to use this type of terminal, you may have to consult with your system administrator for instructions about connecting to the UNIX system.

Logging In

Most UNIX installations use a security system, which requires users to identify themselves. Before you can begin to use UNIX, you have to be able to access it, and so the first thing to learn is how to let UNIX know you want to become an active user. This process is called *logging in*.

UNIX controls access to the system with a program called **login**. The system administrator assigns users of the system *user names* (or *logons*) and *passwords*, which identify them to the UNIX system. Usually each user name is unique, but sometimes a group of people who perform similar tasks on the computer will share a common name. Each user name refers to an *account* in UNIX terminology.

User names are usually related to the users' real names, but each system administrator will have his or her own naming convention. Some use the first letter of the first name with the last name (e.g., tparker), or initials (tjp), or simply the first name (tim). In many small companies, first names are used to make the system more informal, but this can cause problems when people share the same first name. Larger systems with many users may use complex logons that sometimes do not bear any resemblance to the user's name, but simplify accounting and tracking purposes.

User names and passwords normally appear in lowercase, according to UNIX convention. The system administrator may change this, but case is important to the UNIX operating system, so you must always use care to ensure you are entering names and passwords in the correct case.

The **login** program's task is to control access by requiring users to identify themselves. This allows **login** to execute specific commands for that user, and to know where the user's *home directory* is located. (We will discuss home directories later in this chapter.) In cases where users are billed for access time, the **login** program initiates an entry to the accounting log.

When the **login** program is active, it displays a message on terminals connected to the computer. The prompt may be different on some systems, as it can be changed by the system administrator, but usually it appears as follows:

```
login:
```

When this message is displayed, **login** is waiting for the user to type a name. After you type your user name, press the Return key to send the name to the computer. **login** usually responds with the prompt:

```
Password:
```

and waits for the user to enter the correct password for the user name. If a password is not required, then this prompt does not appear. After entering your password, press Return. While you enter your password, **login** shuts off the screen echo of what you type so the password is not displayed. You should therefore take care to enter your password correctly.

When you are typing your user name or password, you can correct errors with the backspace key. If you press Return after making an error, though, you will have to press Return again to force **login** to re-display the prompt

login. login compares the user name and password you enter against a table of all existing entries. If it finds a match, you are allowed access to the UNIX system. If either the name or the password doesn't match, **login** responds with a message similar to:

```
Login incorrect
```

and re-displays the **login** prompt.

If the system fails to recognize the user name and password again, check to make sure the Caps Lock key is not on, as this would force all the letters to the opposite case. If you still don't succeed in logging in, inform the system administrator. Chances are that the account was set with a different user name and password from the ones you tried.

Some UNIX systems will allow you to log in using uppercase user names and passwords. These systems were originally designed to work with older terminals that did not have lowercase characters. If you do log in successfully in uppercase, UNIX will think that you are using one of these older terminals, and your screen will probably be filled with garbage before too long. The best thing to do is to log out and start again, making sure you are using lowercase. When you have logged in to the UNIX system, several things may happen. Depending on how the administrator has set up the system, you may be presented immediately with a menu, or you may get a message from the system, followed by a dollar sign ($) or percent sign (%). Alternatively, you may get this system prompt:

```
TERM=(unknown)
```

If this prompt is displayed, simply press Return for now, and you should see either the dollar sign, or the percent sign. These two signs are called *shell prompt characters*, and they identify the shell you are using. We will discuss shells later (they are the interface between you and the UNIX system).

Before you see the shell prompt character, you may get a few lines of text shown on the screen. This is called the "message of the day" (UNIX, which likes to abbreviate everything, calls this **motd**), and it is displayed whenever you log on. The system administrator can change this message, and usually uses it to warn you when the system will be down, when changes to the system have been made, or other important news.

You may also, just above the shell prompt character, get the message:

    You have mail.

This is generated by UNIX's mail package, and tells you that you have something waiting in your mailbox.

Logging Out

To leave UNIX, you can use one of several commands. The easiest method is to press Ctrl-D (hold down Ctrl and press the 'd' key). This sends a termination signal to UNIX, and the system ends your session. The **login** prompt should reappear.

Some systems disable the Ctrl-D sequence to prevent users from accidentally logging out. If so, one of two commands will accomplish the same task. If the dollar sign is used as the prompting character, then you can type the command **exit** (in lowercase) and press Return. If the percent sign is the prompting character, type the command **logout** and press Return. The **login** prompt should be re-displayed.

It is important that you always remember to log out of the system when you are finished with it. If you leave the terminal while still logged in, someone else may use the system and have access to all your files. They may cause damage, or make unwanted changes.

In addition, if the system bills for account usage, you will be charged as long as you are logged on. Leaving the system without logging out allows someone else to use it, with you paying the bill!

Whether accounts are charged or not, it is good to establish the habit of logging out whenever you are finished, or even when you are leaving for a few minutes, if the terminal is in a readily accessible place. Most users have some files they consider personal, and staying logged in invites others to snoop!

Identifying Your Terminal

UNIX can communicate with a wide range of terminals. Because it does not always know what kind of terminal you are using, it may ask you to tell it. If the terminal is always in place, the system administrator may have already told UNIX the terminal type, and you will not have to worry about it.

When you log in, if you get a system prompt that looks like this:

    TERM=(unknown)

then UNIX wants you to identify the type of terminal you are using. (There may be something else in the parentheses instead of "unknown".) All terminals are identified to UNIX by a short-form name. The Wyse 60 terminal, for example, is called "wyse60" or "wy60". The Qume QVT 101+ terminal is called "qvt101+". If you do not know the terminal type, it is important to find out. An application that runs on your terminal uses this information to tell it how to send characters to the screen, and if the information is incorrect, you may wind up with a hopeless mess.

When you know the terminal's short-form name, you can type it at the **TERM** prompt. If there is a name in parentheses after the prompt, the system is using a default name and is asking you to confirm the type. If, for example, you are on a Digital Equipment VT-100 terminal, and the system displays the prompt:

    TERM=(vt100)

all you need to do is press Return to confirm the type. If the terminal type is incorrect, or is "unknown", you must enter it correctly. Remember to use lowercase, as this is the convention (unless otherwise instructed by the system administrator).

If the terminal type has been entered correctly, the system will either continue to display a message and the prompting character, or execute a program automatically.

If the terminal type has been supplied incorrectly, the system responds with a prompt similar to:

> unknown terminal type

or

> type termname unknown

where "termname" is the name you entered. UNIX then displays the prompting character. However, the UNIX system has not managed to identify the instructions your terminal needs, and a screenfull of garbage may be the result at some point if you proceed without correctly identifying the terminal.

It is possible to change the terminal type while at the prompt character, using a simple instruction. Suppose you are using a Wyse 60 terminal, but misspelled the short-form name when entering it. At the prompt character, you can enter the following:

> TERM=wyse60; export TERM

using the correct terminal type. The first part tells UNIX that the system variable TERM is to be given the new name. (TERM is a variable used by UNIX to hold the short-form name of your terminal.) The **export** command tells UNIX to assign that name to the system variable. Without the **export** command, no change in terminal type occurs. The semicolon identifies a new command. You could just as easily type the commands on two separate lines:

> TERM=wyse60
> export TERM

and accomplish the same thing, but keeping them all on the same line tends to marry the two steps in the user's mind. Note that the **TERM** command is typed in uppercase characters to identify it as a system variable, but **export** must be lowercase!

Many terminals have *emulation modes*. It is entirely possible to be using a Wyse 60 terminal, but enter the name "vt100" for the terminal type. This simply means that the Wyse is assuming the same command set as the Digital Equipment VT-100 terminal. Most UNIX systems have a long list of supported terminals, so be sure to check that you have the correct terminal type.

Beginning to Use UNIX

You know the two most important things a user needs to know about a UNIX system: how to get on it, and how to get off! Now you can begin to use some commands and build up experience on the system.

If something goes wrong, or you mistype a command, just try it again when you get the shell prompt character. UNIX will give you a message if you have spelled a command wrong, or if you try to do something it doesn't want you to do.

The Shell

UNIX is an operating system. It doesn't really know how to communicate with a user. Instead, it uses application software to do this. Most people think application software only means spreadsheets, word processors, databases, and other programs of this kind. But there are many other application programs that most users don't think of in this way, even though they use them every day.

The first application program a user sees is **login**, which we discussed in the previous section. This program lets you get into another application program, called the *shell*. The "shell" is a generic name for an interface program, which sits between the UNIX operating system and the user. It performs many tasks, but its main one is to allow the user to access the operating system without knowing anything about UNIX programming. Without the shell, a user would have to write programs to accomplish most simple tasks!

It is very unusual for users not to use a shell when they log in. The most common exception is when a specific program is loaded instead of the shell, which controls what the user can do. But even such a program can be thought of as a shell.

The shell is used to run all the other applications on the system, and it provides a common interface for other programs. The shell is a complicated program with several built-in utilities that other programs can use. Another application, such as a word processor, will be loaded over the shell and may make use of some features of the shell.

The shell also provides a way for users to perform programming tasks that alter the user interface without having to know a programming language. The shell "language" is comparatively simple and easy to learn. We will be using many shell commands throughout this book.

Because different users may want to interact with the operating system in different ways, several types of shells have been designed. The original and most common shell is called the Bourne shell. Many programmers who write in the C language use a special shell called the C Shell because it behaves like C. Newer, more elaborate shells are also available.

For now, it is enough to know that each shell uses one or more characters on the screen to tell the user that it is loaded and waiting for a command. This character (the shell prompt character already mentioned) can be changed by the user, but it is usually the dollar sign ($) for the Bourne shell and the percent sign (%) for the C shell. All the commands you will learn in this book work in both shells, so it really doesn't matter which you are using.

Is Anyone Out There? (The **who** Command)

UNIX allows users to identify the other currently logged-in users of the system with the **who** command. This can be useful for determining if a colleague is using the computer, or if the system is under a heavy load, and for avoiding a conflict in accessing system resources.

A number of options that can be used with the **who** command to provide different information. If you enter the **who** command by itself at the shell prompt, it provides a list of current users:

```
$who
tim        tty01      Jun 20   10:52
bill       tty83      Jun 20   09:45
deb        tty8a      Jun 20   07:35
$
```

Each one of the names shown is a user name. Each line also shows the terminal number the user is on (as it is identified by the UNIX system) as well as the date and time the user logged on. With a system like the example shown, which uses first names, it is likely that only a few users actually use the system at once and you will know them all. But on a large system, the number of users can be very large, and you may not know any of the other users.

Changing Your Password (The *passwd* Command)

It is a very good idea to change your password when you are starting to use the system, and to change it several times throughout the year. This ensures that you are the only one who knows your password. Some systems may force you to change your password at preselected intervals.

You change your password with a UNIX program called **passwd**. UNIX uses a lot of commands that are simply contractions or abbreviations of longer words, and this makes them easier to remember.

When you log on to the system and see the shell prompt character, enter:

```
$passwd
```

and the system will tell you it is changing your password and ask you to enter your old password:

```
Changing password for tim
Old password:
```

Your user name appears in the place of "tim", of course. The system does the password check as a security check, just in case someone else tries to change your password. When you have typed in your old password and press Return, UNIX responds with:

```
Enter new password (minimum of 5 characters)
Please use a combination of upper and lowercase letters and numbers.
New password:
```

at which point you can type in your new password. After you have entered it, UNIX asks you to enter it again to make sure there are no errors that may prevent you from getting access again:

```
Re-enter new password:
```

If you enter two different passwords, UNIX sends you a message similar to this:

```
They don't match; try again.
```

You must then try the process all over again. When you type the same password twice, the shell prompt character reappears. UNIX does not give you a message to say that you have completed the command successfully. You may as well get used to this now: UNIX sends the user very few messages—only when absolutely necessary.

The next time you log in, you will have to use your new password. It is not a good idea to write a password down because someone else might find it. Also, it is best not to use passwords that can be guessed easily. Many users have passwords consisting of their spouses' or children's names, their pets' names, or birthdays. All of these can be guessed easily by someone else.

Instead, try choosing a word that is not directly related to you. Such a password can be anything, but it is easier to remember "spring" than "736jbhs"! In general, try to make your passwords at least six characters long, and don't be obvious.

Testing, Testing...

Before we really delve into files and directories, we should try some other UNIX commands to better understand the shell interface.

First, we'll deliberately make a mistake. At the shell prompt, type a random string of characters that do not spell anything sensible, press Return, and see if UNIX understands what you typed. Unless you were extremely lucky and typed the name of a UNIX command, you should see something like this:

```
$qwerty
qwerty: not found
$
```

UNIX is telling you that it could not find a command called "qwerty", and that it doesn't understand what it means.

Now try a valid command. We'll check today's date and time using the UNIX **date** command. At the shell prompt, enter "date":

```
$date
Sat June 22 10:25:16 EST 1989
$
```

The program responds with its current information. Many systems are inaccurate with their time, for various reasons, so do not be too surprised if the time displayed is off by a little!

Remember that case is very important to UNIX. If you had typed "DATE" in uppercase letters, you would have gotten the "not found" message again. It is very easy to hit the Caps Lock key accidentally on most keyboards, so you should check this if there is a problem.

UNIX allows you to type several commands on a single line, as long as they are separated by semicolons. To demonstrate this, type:

```
$date; who
```

You should get the date and then a list of the users on the system, as we did before.

Summary

In this chapter, you have seen how to log in and out of the UNIX system, and how to identify your terminal correctly. You have also seen a couple of UNIX commands that can be used at the shell prompt character. You can now use this information as a basis upon which to build your knowledge of the UNIX system. The commands we have used in this chapter are summarized in Table 2.1.

Table 2.1: Summary of Commands

Command	Description
date	displays system date and time
export	sets a UNIX variable (like **TERM**)
passwd	changes your password
TERM	defines your terminal type
who	lists all users currently on the system

Chapter 3

Managing Files and Directories Efficiently

Using Files

UNIX saves all the information it handles as *files*, which it stores on devices such as hard disks. Databases, spreadsheet applications, word-processed documents, executable programs, and all other types of information that must be retained for future access are kept on storage devices as streams of information identified by unique file names. Files can be short, consisting of one byte, or very large, storing many megabytes of data.

When information is written to the storage medium (we will use a hard disk as the example throughout this chapter), UNIX allocates disk space for the file, and then identifies it in an internal table with the file name.

Each user can have many files. Unlike operating systems like DOS, UNIX allows a great deal of versatility in naming the files. For example, DOS only allows up to eight characters in file names, plus a three-character extension as the extension (usually a description of the file type), but UNIX allows a lot more than that. The exact number of characters permitted in a valid UNIX file name depends on the version of UNIX being used, but is typically about twenty-five. These characters can be almost any valid character on your keyboard. The file names "source_code_for_program" and "Silly-file name" are both valid. The fact that UNIX differentiates between upper and lowercase causes some confusion for users accustomed to operating systems that do not. In other words, "TestFile", "testfile" and "Testfile" are all treated as different file names by UNIX.

Getting a List of Your Files (The l Command)

First, we'll use the **who** UNIX command to create a file for us. After you have logged in and the shell prompt character is showing on your terminal, enter the following command:

```
$who > user.list
```

We have already used the **who** command to list the users of the system. The ">" character tells UNIX to redirect the output from the **who** command to the specified file. For this reason, UNIX refers to the ">" symbol as the *redirect* symbol. The command you typed tells UNIX to take the output from the **who** command, which normally would be shown on the screen, and redirect it into a file called "user.list".

To see a list of files, you enter the command l (for list). You should have the shell prompt character showing on your screen after the redirection command has finished. Now type the command for a list of files:

```
$l
```

and the system should respond with a list of files, like this:

```
$l
total 2
-rw-r--r--   1     tim   group   128   Jun 20 10:59 user.list
$
```

More files may be listed, but one of them will be "user.list" if the redirection was completed properly.

If you received a message like this:

```
$l
l: not found
```

then your version of UNIX does not support the l command. Instead, you will have to use the command **ls -l** which accomplishes the same thing. The hyphen before the second "l" is important, as it indicates that the "l" is part of the command. You can try the **ls** command alone without the "-l", and see the difference.

Even if the l command gives the correct result, you can still use the **ls -l** command. The result is the same, but the **ls** format is a little longer to type. If your system does not support l you will have to remember to use **ls -l** whenever we refer to l.

The information the l command gives on each line tells you a lot about the files. From left to right, the elements indicate the following:

```
$l
-rw-rw-r--           file permissions
1                    number of links
tim                  owner of the file
group                the group the owner is in
128                  size of the file in bytes
Jun 20 10:59         date and time the file was saved
user.list            name of the file
```

We will discuss file permissions later in this chapter. The owner of the file should be the same as the name you used to log in, since you are the one who created it. The time and date will tell you exactly when the "user.list" file was written to the disk. The size of the file is always given in bytes.

If you were to redirect the information from the **who** command to the same file name again, and then issue another l command, you would see that the time has changed to reflect the time of the second **who** command.

```
$who > user.list
$l
total 2
-rw-r--r--   1    tim  group  105  Jun 20 11:00 user.list
$
```

Notice that in our example, the file's size has dropped, because there are fewer users now than there were earlier.

You may have also noticed one important fact about UNIX. It did not bother to let you know that there was already a file called "user.list" on the disk. Instead, it simply went ahead and erased the previous file, and saved the new one with the same name. UNIX does not warn users about duplicate file names. It assumes you know what you are doing, and that you intended to overwrite the old file. For this reason, you have to be very careful when saving information under new file names to ensure you do not overwrite valuable information!

Now create two new files using the same command but different file names, and then list the directory again, as shown here:

```
$who > newuser.list
$who > user.newlist
$l
total 6
-rw-r--r--   1    tim    group   110   Jun 20 11:01 newuser.list
-rw-r--r--   1    tim    group   105   Jun 20 11:00 user.list
-rw-r--r--   1    tim    group   110   Jun 20 11:01 user.newlist
$
```

Most versions of UNIX have an abbreviated listing command called **lc**. This stands for 'list columnar', but is often thought of as 'list compressed'. This command will sort the file names alphabetically and display them in columns:

```
$lc
newuser.list    user.list        user.newlist
$
```

The **lc** command does not provide information about the file sizes or save dates, but it does give a cleaner, easier to read directory listing. (Many DOS users who use the "dir /w" command will prefer **lc**, as it presents information in a familiar format.)

The **l** and **lc** commands can each be entered with an *argument* to specify particular file names. If you specify a file name in full, then only that file will be displayed:

```
$l user.list
-rw-r--r--   1    tim   group   105   Jun 20 11:00 user.list
$lc user.list
user.list
$
```

UNIX also supports the use of *wildcard characters* to match one or more letters in a name. A single asterisk (*) alone matches all characters. Therefore, the command:

```
$l *
```

is the same as typing the command without the asterisk. The most commonly used wildcard character is an asterisk. You can use an asterisk to match specific patterns. For example, the command:

```
$l u*
```

will list all files whose names begin with the letter "u", no matter how long or involved the file names are.

Along the same lines, the command:

```
$l user*
```

will list all those that begin with "user".

The question mark (?) is another "wildcard" character, but it an only be used to match single characters. The command:

```
$l use?
```

will list only those file names that begin with "use" and have a single fourth character. File names longer than four characters will not be displayed. We could list only those file names that are four characters long with the command:

```
$l ????
```

The two wildcard characters can be used together to display specific patterns. For example, the command:

    $l ?ser*

will display all file names of four characters or more whose second, third and fourth characters are "ser".

We will discuss wildcards and the listing commands further at a later point in this chapter.

Displaying Your Files (The **cat** and **more** Commands)

UNIX allows you to examine the contents of a file in several ways. One of the more basic methods uses a command that provides considerable power for file manipulation, so we will discuss that first, and introduce a straightforward file display method.

To begin the process, simply enter:

    $ cat user.list

UNIX responds by displaying the contents of the file. Naturally, the content of your file will be different, but it will have a format similar to this:

```
$cat user.list
tim          tty01       Jun 20 10:52
mike         tty82       Jun 20 10:56
bill         tty83       Jun 20 09:45
bob          tty86       Jun 20 11:00
deb          tty8a       Jun 20 07:35
$
```

The UNIX **cat** command (short for concatenate) will show the contents of the file. In this case, we haven't given **cat** any instruction to tell it where to put the contents, so it lists it to the screen (the default). When UNIX has listed the entire contents of the file, the shell prompt reappears.

You can use the **cat** command to display many files, one after the other. For example, if you issue the command:

    $cat user.list newuser.list

UNIX will display the contents of both files. You can list many file names, as long as you separate them each by at least one space.

You can also use **cat** to copy files with the UNIX redirection symbol. The command:

```
$ cat user.list > test.file
```

tells UNIX to **cat** the file "user.list", and to redirect the output into another file, called "test.file". You can just as easily combine multiple files into one file by using both of the last techniques together:

```
$ cat user.list newuser.list > two.files
```

The new file "two.files" will have the contents of both "user.list" and "newuser.list" one after the other. If you use the **cat** command to display these files, you can verify this for yourself.

If your system has many users, the output on your terminal screen may occupy more than the terminal's number of lines. If that is the case, the data will scroll from top to bottom, and new lines that appear at the bottom will force the top lines to disappear.

UNIX allows you to stop this scrolling with a special sequence. If you are **cat**ting a file, and want to halt it during the process, hold down the Ctrl key and press "s". The scrolling should stop. To start it again, press Ctrl-Q. It is convenient to think of Ctrl-s as "s"topping the scroll. Ctrl-Q is more difficult, but some users think of it as "q"uitting the stop.

Some terminals have special keys labeled Scroll Lock that will send the Ctrl-S and Ctrl-Q combinations automatically. If you are not sure, ask an experienced user or your system administrator.

Although **cat** allows you to redirect files, add files together, and send the output to a number of different devices, it does not present information on the screen in a clean way. Instead, **cat** simply "throws" the file's contents to the screen, and leaves it up to the user to stop and start the screen display.

Most versions of UNIX have a screen-oriented file display program called **more**. This program will use the information it has about your terminal to display files one full screen at a time.

If the file to be displayed has less than one screenful of information, **more** acts very much like **cat**: It simply shows the information line by line, and then presents you with another shell prompt character. But if the file has more than one screenful of information, then **more** really becomes useful. To illustrate this, we will use **more** to display the contents of a system file called **termcap** that contains all the definitions with which UNIX identifies terminal types. At the shell prompt, enter the following:

```
$more /etc/termcap
```

The program will clear your screen, and display the first screenful of the file. The contents of the file will depend upon the version of UNIX, but the file lists a number of terminals, their short identifier names, and definitions for various terminal attributes.

At the bottom of the screen, the prompt:

```
--More--(1%)
```

will be shown. The figure shown in the parentheses is the percentage of the entire file that you have passed at the bottom of the screen. It will vary with each copy of **termcap.**

The **more** program has a number of commands that can be used to perform different tasks when displaying a file. The easiest task is to move to the next screen, which is accomplished by simply pressing the Spacebar. Each time you do so, the next screen is displayed, until the file has been completely shown. You cannot move backwards through a file; **more** only allows display from top to bottom.

To exit the **more** program, you can simply type **q** (quit), and the shell prompt character will be displayed. Another way to exit on many terminals is to press the **Del** key, but this will depend on how your terminal has been set up.

You can also use a special key to find text in a file that is being displayed by **more**. The slash character (/) is used to tell **more** that you want to search for the string of characters after the slash. If you still have the **termcap** file displayed on the screen, type:

    /wy50

to tell **more** to search for the string "wy50". (This is the short-form name for a Wyse 50 terminal.) The top of the screen displays the message:

    ...skipping

as the **more** program examines the file from the current location to the end to find the requested character string. If it doesn't manage to find the string, it will display the same screen as before, but the bottom will read:

    Pattern not found

If **more** does find the string, it displays the part of the screen in which the string occurs.

Deleting Your Files (The **rm** Command)   (del)

Earlier, you created some files with **cat**, so now you may wish to delete a few files in your area. To delete a file, use the **rm** (remove) command. It's very simple to use:

    $rm two.files

As you might expect by now, UNIX does not display any message to show that it has completed the deletion, but a list of your files would show that it is indeed gone.

The "wildcards" that you learned earlier can be used with **rm**. For example, you could have issued the command:

    $rm two.*

or the command:

```
$rm *.files
```

to accomplish the same task. The first version would also have deleted any other files that started with "two.". The second would have deleted any files that ended with ".files".

The **rm** command has an option that you can use to prevent deleting files inadvertently. This is accomplished by using the **-i** (interactive) option with the command, for example:

```
$rm -i two.*
```

With the command in this format, **rm** will pause before deleting each file and ask you to confirm that you want to delete it. Answering "y" will cause the file to be deleted, or "n" will not delete the file and **rm** will display the next file that matches the name. Although you can use the **-i** option with a single file name:

```
$rm -i two.files
```

or even multiple file names:

```
$rm -i two.files newuser.list
```

there is no reason to do so because in each case you have already typed the names of the files. The interactive option is most useful with wildcards. You can use it to clean up the files in an entire directory as follows:

```
$rm -i *
```

The asterisk will match every file name in your directory. And the **-i** tells UNIX to query you before deleting each one.

This also brings up a useful warning. The command:

```
$rm *
```

without the **-i** argument erases everything in a directory without asking you to confirm, and with UNIX it is almost impossible to "unerase" files that have been deleted. Therefore, be very careful when using the "rm *" command.

If you tell UNIX to **rm** a file that doesn't exist, it will give you a message back to say it couldn't find that file.

Renaming Your Files (The *mv* Command)

UNIX allows you to rename a file using the **mv** (move) command. While **mv** is normally used to move files from one area of the hard disk to another, it can just as easily be used to change the name of a file.

To try an example, first create a new file with the **who** command:

    $who > new.file

Then rename "new.file" to "old.file" using the following command:

    $mv new.file old.file

As with most UNIX commands, **mv** does not give you any message that the task has been completed successfully, except for the return of the shell prompt character. You can use the l command to verify that the proper action has occurred.

Copying Your Files (The *cp* Command)

Files are copied in several ways on a UNIX system. You already know that you can create a copy of a file by using the **cat** command and redirecting its output to the new file name. UNIX also supplies a special copy command, called **cp**, to perform the same action. To copy "old.file" to "older.file", you issue the **cp** command in its simplest form:

    $cp old.file older.file

Both files will have identical contents.

File Permissions

Each file on a UNIX system has a special set of attributes to tell UNIX who created the file, and who has access to it. By using these attributes (called *permissions*) UNIX knows when to allow a user to modify a file, and whether it can be executed as a program.

Each file's permissions are displayed when the l command is issued. The display of files looks something like this:

```
-rw-r--r--  1    tim  group  110  Jun 20 11:01 newuser.list
-rw-r--r--  1    tim  group  105  Jun 20 11:00 user.list
-rw-r--r--  1    tim  group  110  Jun 20 11:01 user.newlist
```

The permissions are the first items listed for each file, and occupy ten characters of the line.

The first character indicates the *type* of file. There are quite a few valid characters for the file type, but most users generally encounter only a few of them.

If the type character is a hyphen (-) it indicates an ordinary file. A "d" indicates a directory name. (We will discuss directories shortly.) Most users will see only these two types, regardless of the amount of work they do on the system. The other types are encountered by system administrators and system programmers.

The next nine characters are used to show the permissions the file has. Permissions for UNIX are divided into three sets, one each for the owner, the group, and all users. The "owner" is the person who created or last modified the file. The "group" is a category to which the system administrator can assign users.

Each one of the three sets of permissions is broken down into three specific types of permission. The first character of the first set will be **r** if the owner has read permission or - if the owner does not. The second will be **w** if the owner has write permission or - if not. The third character will be **x** if the owner has execute permission, or - if not. The next three are broken down the same way for the group, and the last three are for all users. As an example, for the following file:

```
-rw-rw-r--   1    tim   group   110  Jun 20 11:01 user.newlist
```

the first permissions character shows that the file type is ordinary. The next three characters "rw-" indicate that the owner of the file (in this case "tim"), has read and write permissions for this file, but not execute permission. (That is, the file is not executable, so the third character is -.) The group that "tim" belongs to (in this case "group") likewise has read and write ("rw") permission, but all other users have only read permission (shown by the "r--").

Only those with write permission can change the contents of a file, although anyone with read permission can look at it. If users who don't have read permission try to look at the file, copy it, delete it, or try some other UNIX command on it, they will get a message denying them access.

File permissions can be changed by the file's owner, and by those who have a higher level of access on the system (such as the system administrator).

Redirection and Piping

You have already used the redirection character when you issued the "who > user.list" command. The ">" character signifies that UNIX is to redirect the output of the command to the specified location.

In this case, as we saw, it will erase whatever was in the file name we have specified and overwrite it with the new information.

UNIX also allows you to append the information from a new command into an existing file. This is done with two redirection characters, as the following command sequence demonstrates:

```
$who > newfile
$who >> newfile
```

Now, if you display the contents of "newfile" with either **cat** or **more**, you will see that it does indeed contain the output from the **who** command two times.

Thus, you can either redirect or append the ouput of UNIX commands. In fact, redirection is one of the really strong features of UNIX from a programming point of view.

Suppose you want to issue a command that generates so much output that it would rapidly scroll by on the screen. You already know that **more** is useful for displaying files, but you can also send the output of a command to **more**. This is known as *piping* (you are "piping" the output of one command to the input of another), and is accomplished with the vertical bar symbol "|". The following sends the output of the **who** command to **more** so that it will be displayed cleanly on the screen:

```
$who | more
```

(Remember that if there is less than one screenful of information, **more** will not really have any effect. It will just display the information and then issue a shell prompt character.) This "piping" accomplishes the same task as redirecting the output of a command to a temporary file, then displaying the temporary file, and then deleting it.

If you had a lot of files in your file area, and they scrolled by the screen when an l was performed, you could pipe the output of the l command to the **more** command using:

```
$l | more
```

and get a screen-by-screen display of your files.

Piping is not only done to the **more** command. You can pipe any output to any program that expects input. You will see other examples of this as we continue through the UNIX system.

Organizing Your Work with Directories

Most DOS users are familiar with directories and subdirectories. These concepts were derived from UNIX, which uses a very similar structure for its directory layout. Also, directory commands are basically the same for UNIX and DOS.

One major difference, which those familiar with DOS will have to get used to, is that UNIX uses the slash character (/) as a separator instead of the backslash (\).

As you will see, many of the commands used with directories are similar or exactly the same as those we used for files. This is because UNIX thinks of directories as files, which simplifies the whole process for us.

The Directory Structure

If all the files on a multiuser system were stored in one place, they would very rapidly grow unmanageable. Determining who owned which files, and what each file related to would become a rather complicated process. In order to solve this problem, UNIX allows a user to create special areas, called *directories*, on the hard disk that are identified by particular names. Each directory can itself hold files and other directories.

It is often convenient to think of directories as a hierarchy in the shape of an inverted tree. The base area of the UNIX system is called the "root" directory and is signified by the slash symbol "/". A sample directory structure is shown in Figure 3.1 on the next page.

Below the root directory, UNIX creates several other directories for specific purposes. There is usually a directory called "bin", for example, that holds executable files ("bin" stands for "binary"). The "dev" directory (device) holds special information about all the devices (terminals, modems, printers, and so on) attached to the UNIX system. The "etc" directory holds a number of UNIX programs.

40 UNIX SURVIVAL GUIDE

Figure 3.1: A Sample Directory Structure

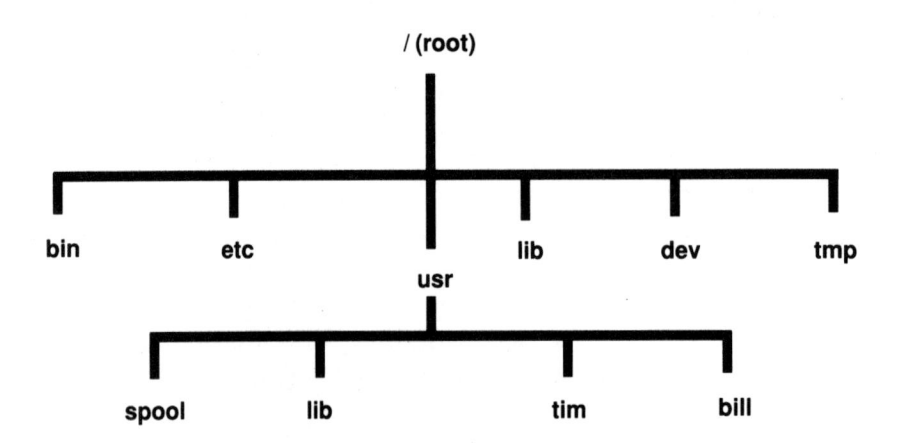

```
                         / (root)
        ┌────────┬──────────┼──────────┬────────┐
       bin      etc        lib        dev      tmp
                         usr
                ┌─────────┼─────────┐
              spool      lib       tim       bill
```

A UNIX system will usually also have a special directory called "usr" (or sometimes just "u") that is dedicated to storing system users' files. Below the "usr" directory will be another directory level for each system user.

UNIX does not limit the number of directories a system can have. Each directory can itself have many directories beneath it.

Users' Home Directories (The *pwd* Command)

Each user on a UNIX system is assigned a directory when the system administrator creates their account. This directory usually has a two-part name, such as "usr/tim". The part of the name after the slash, which in this example is "tim", will be the same as the user's login name. The part before the slash identifies a directory in the UNIX system, and is typically either "usr" or "u", depending on how the system administrator set up the system.

When you are logged on to the UNIX system, you are automatically placed in your assigned directory. In UNIX terms, this is called your *home directory*.

The home directory is the default area to which you save any files unless you (or the application you are running) specify otherwise.

UNIX has a command to allow you to display the name of the directory you are currently in, called **pwd** (print working directory). If you are logged in, try this at the shell prompt:

```
$pwd
/usr/tim
$
```

Usually, UNIX assumes when you tell it a file name it is in the current directory, unless you specify otherwise. For example, if you wanted to get a file called "test.file" from another user's directory called "usr/joe", you would have to identify the file as "/usr/joe/test.file".

Each file in your home directory can be called either by its individual name, or by its full name, which includes the directory information. The file "user.list", which you created in your home directory earlier, is really called "/usr/tim/user.list" (with your user name instead of "tim".) When you used the **more** command to display the contents of this file, you typed:

```
$more user.list
```

but you could also have entered:

```
$more /usr/tim/user.list
```

if your home directory had been "/usr/tim".

Your home directory is unique to you, as the UNIX system normally does not allow two people to have the same user name. (It is possible that several people will share a user name, and hence have the same home directory, but this is rare.)

The name of your home directory is assigned as a special variable in UNIX called HOME. Whenever a command that refers to a directory sees the name HOME, it will substitute the full name of the home directory for you. This is useful when writing programs that many people will use, releasing you from having to account for all the home directory names in full.

Moving About Directories (The cd Command)

UNIX lets you move through different directories, as long as you have access to them. You do this with the **cd** command (change directory). Regardless of where you are on the UNIX system, you can always get back to your home directory by typing the **cd** command by itself. Suppose you were in a directory called "tmp", and you wanted to go back to your home directory. You could simply type **cd**. In the example below, we first change to the "tmp" directory and then back to the home directory:

```
$cd /tmp
$pwd
/tmp
$cd
$pwd
/usr/tim
```

The **cd** command allows you to move throughout the UNIX file system at will. At the shell prompt, you can move from your home directory ("usr/tim" for example) to the parent directory ("usr") in one of two ways. You can tell it the name of the directory you want to go to explicitly:

```
$pwd
/usr/tim
$cd /usr
$pwd
/usr
$
```

Another way to move "up" a level is by using a special command to signify the "parent" of the directory you are currently in. The parent is simply the next level higher in the directory structure toward the root system. UNIX uses a special symbol to signify the "parent": two periods in a row. If you move back to the home directory by issuing the **cd** command by itself, you can get to the "/usr" directory again with the "parent" instruction:

```
$cd
$pwd
/usr/tim
$cd ..
$pwd
/usr
$
```

The two-period (..) short form for the parent directory saves you a lot of typing. UNIX also has an abbreviated way to indicate the current directory: a single period before a slash. The commands:

```
$l *.list
```

and

```
$l ./*.list
```

both refer to files in the current directory. You will have to be careful not to confuse the period for the current directory with the period in the file name after the asterisk. Remember that when the directory is being referred to, the period is followed by the slash.

Creating Directories Yourself (The **mkdir** Command)

If you do a lot of work that falls logically into a group, you can place all this work in a directory you create yourself. As an example, assume you were writing a book on UNIX, and each chapter had its own file. It would make sense to place the entire contents of the book in a directory of its own, underneath your home directory.

UNIX allows you to create directories using the **mkdir** (make directory) command. To check that you are in your home directory and then create a directory called "unixbook" under it, you would issue the following commands:

```
$cd
$pwd
/usr/tim
$l
$mkdir unixbook
```

```
-rw-r--r--   1    tim    group   110  Jun 20 11:01 newuser.list
drwxr-wr-w   2    tim    group    32  Jun 20 11:14 unixbook
-rw-r--r--   1    tim    group   105  Jun 20 11:00 user.list
-rw-r--r--   1    tim    group   110  Jun 20 11:01 user.newlist
$cd unixbook
$pwd
/usr/tim/unixbook
$
```

Now that you have created a new directory under the home directory, you can use this area to save all the chapters of the book. You will see the directory name in your listing of files, with the letter "d" as the file type (first character in the permissions) to signify it is a directory. Initially the directory will have nothing in it, but as the book is written, the files that represent chapters will all be placed here.

If you need to, you can create further directories underneath the one you have just created. Suppose you are going to be using a CAD (computer aided design) package to draw diagrams, but you want to keep them separate from the files that represent the chapters. You can create another directory under the "unixbook" directory called "diagrams":

```
$pwd
/usr/tim/unixbook
$mkdir diagrams
$l
total 2
drwxr-xr-x   2    tim    group    32  Jun 20 11:15 diagrams
$
```

Figure 3.2 on the following page shows the new directory structure.

You could continue creating directories as needed, but bear in mind that having too many divisions tends to make the file system unwieldy and awkward to navigate.

Usually, directories are created for distinct subjects that can be separated from other material. Grouping similar material together can make it easier to locate files, especially if you use descriptive names for the directories. As with all UNIX files, you can call a directory practically anything you want, so it is often useful to use descriptive names. (On the other hand, remember that you will have to type the names, so don't make them too long!)

Figure 3.2: A Home Directory with Subdirectories

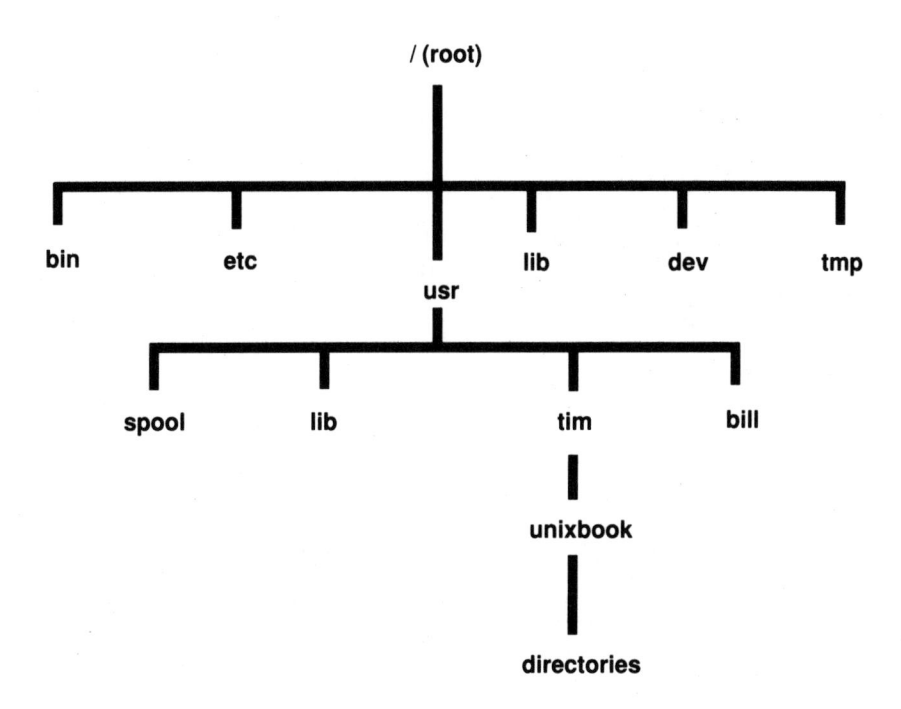

```
                           / (root)
         ┌──────┬──────┬─────┼─────┬──────┬──────┐
        bin    etc          usr   lib    dev    tmp
                       ┌──────┼──────┬──────┐
                      spool  lib    tim    bill
                                     │
                                  unixbook
                                     │
                                 directories
```

Removing Your Directories (The *rmdir* Command)

You just created a directory called something like "usr/tim/unixbook/diagrams". Now suppose you realize that you won't be making diagrams after all. To keep the file structure neat and clear of useless directories, remove it from your directory tree using the **rmdir** (remove directory) command:

```
$cd /usr/tim/unixbook
$pwd
/usr/tim/unixbook
$l
total 2
```

```
drwxr-xr-x    2      tim    group     32   Jun 20 11:15 diagrams
$rmdir diagrams
$l
total 0
$
```

The **rmdir** command performs a check of the directory you are trying to remove first, and if there are any files still in it, it returns a message like this:

```
$rmdir diagrams
rmdir: diagrams not empty
$
```

Before you can completely remove a directory, it must be empty. (You will learn a quick way around this later.) To clean out the directory, change to that directory, perform a **rm** command, using a wildcard (*) to remove all the files, then go back and try **rmdir** again:

```
$cd /usr/tim/unixbook/diagrams
$rm *
$cd/usr/tim/unixbook
$rmdir diagrams
$
```

Copying and Renaming Directories (The *copy* Command)

Renaming directories works the same way as renaming files. You use the **mv** command, and provide the names of the old directory and the new one:

```
$mv unixbook newbook
```

Any files in a directory that you renamed will remain as they were. UNIX automatically recognizes the name change and associates the old files with the new directory name.

Copying files from one directory to another can be done in several ways. The easiest is to use the **copy** command. To copy files from "/usr/tim/newbook" to /usr/tim/backup", for example, you would use the following command:

```
$copy /usr/tim/newbook /usr/tim/backup
```

When this command is executed, all files in the first directory are copied to the second directory, without changing the contents of the first. (Note that if you do not have write access to the second directory, the command will not execute.)

Summary

By now, you should have some real experience using the UNIX system. In this chapter we have covered a lot of material, and you now know:

- how to interpret the file permissions
- how to display files
- how to delete, move, copy and rename files
- how to redirect input and output
- how directory structures work
- how to create new directories
- how to delete, move, rename and copy directories

You now know most of the commands you will ever need to know to use UNIX efficiently! The number of basic commands is not large, and most of them make sense mnemonically. With a little practice, using UNIX will become second nature. The commands we have seen in this chapter are summarized in Table 3.1.

Table 3.1: Summary of Commands

Command	Description
cat	concatenates a file (display or copy)
cd	changes directory
copy	copies files or directories
cp	copies files
l	directory list
lc	columnar directory list
more	displays a file screen by screen
mv	renames (move) a file
pwd	prints current (working) directory
rm	deletes a file
rmdir	removes a directory
who	lists who is currently on the system

Chapter 4

Using Printers and Background Processing

The UNIX system uses printers to allow users to obtain hardcopy of their spreadsheets, word processing documents, database results, and other application output. Instead of using one printer for each user, UNIX allows a large number of users to share one or more printers.

As most users do not need a printer all the time, sharing printers makes sense. UNIX has been designed to handle the management of the printers in a well controlled manner, preventing several users' output from trying to print out at the same time. Instead, UNIX uses a program that places print requests in a queue, and allows them to go by turns to the printer in an ordered manner.

The programs that control the printer all reside in *background* in the UNIX system. In other words, they are not directly controlled by a single user, but are run by the UNIX system itself, and operate continually. The printer programs are transparent to the user: You are never aware that the programs are working. As they run independently, and without interference from users, this kind of program is called a *background process*. Background processes do not interfere with what the user is doing on the terminal.

In this chapter, we will begin by looking at the UNIX printer system, and how you, as a user, can monitor what is going on and control it to some extent. Then, we will examine background processing in general, and see how to send programs into the background and monitor them.

Using a Printer

All UNIX users have the ability to send output to a printer, but few bother to learn how to determine when the output will be printed, and how to cancel the printing if necessary. To get the most out of a UNIX system, being able to handle printers is important, yet easy to do.

In this section, we will examine the printer system used by UNIX, and the commands needed to control the system. There are many more printer commands than we will see here, but those are used by the system administrator, and are not usually available to users. However, there is enough power in the printer commands that are available to users to allow you to do virtually anything you would want to do with printers and print requests.

Sending a File to a Printer (The **lp** and **pr** Commands)

There are several ways to print a file in UNIX, but the easiest way is to use the **lp** (line printer) command. If the file you want to print is called "newfile", issuing the command:

```
$lp newfile
```

sends the file's contents to the printer. UNIX may respond with a single line informing you of the print ID number, which is a number assigned for every print request made on the system. These numbers increment automatically, and provide a unique identifier for each print request. The program **lp** is called the *print spooler*, as it "spools" items to the printers in a queue.

If you get an error message from the system like this:

```
lp: not found
```

then your system does not use the UNIX program called **lp**. It may use one called **lpr**, or have some other name. If you cannot use **lp**, check with your system administrator for the name of the print program your system uses.

In the previous example, we did not specify the printer the file is to be sent to. Each UNIX system has one printer designated as the *default printer*. The default printer is used whenever a different printer name is not specified.

If you do not want to use the default printer, you will have to specify the name of the printer that you do want to use, by using the "- d" option. For example, the command:

    $lp -ddaisy newfile

prints "newfile" on a printer called "daisy".

The **lp** command can accept more than one file at a time, and it can also accept wildcards. The commands:

    $lp newfile oldfile deadfile

and

    $lp *

are both valid instructions to the print spooler. The latter command uses the global wildcard to match all files in the directory.

The **lp** command has several options. The most frequent of these is the **-n** option to indicate more than one copy. The command:

    $lp -n3 newfile

prints three copies of "newfile".

The **-w** option sends the user a message when the files have been successfully printed. The command:

    $lp -w newfile

sends a message to the console that the file has been printed. If the user has logged out since the **lp** command was issued, UNIX sends mail to the user instead. The **-m** option is very similar to the **-w** option, except that it sends mail when the print request has been successfully printed, instead of trying to send a message to the terminal.

A useful command to use with the **lp** command is **pr**, which tells UNIX to paginate the file properly. This prevents the problem of text running off the bottom of the page. In the following example, **pr** paginates "newfile", which is then piped to the command **lp**. **lp** then sends the paginated file to the printer:

```
$pr newfile | lp
```

Sending to a Printer Using Redirection

As with most UNIX devices, printers are treated as files. This allows the use of the UNIX redirection commands. We have seen the use of the pipe earlier, when we directed paginated output to the **lp** program. True redirection is easiest to accomplish with the **cat** (concatenate) command.

To use the UNIX redirection command ">", we need the device name of the printer. To send a file called "newfile" to the main parallel printer with a device name of "/dev/lp1", we can use the command:

```
$cat newfile > /dev/lp1
```

Serial printers will have different device names, so you have to be careful to get the proper name in the command. Otherwise, their user could suddenly get the contents of your file appearing on another terminal!

Getting Printer Status Information

You may occasionally want to check the load a printer has when you have a long document to send, or want to change fonts, printer layout, or other printer parameters. The UNIX **lpstat** command provides a summary of the status of all attached printers. **lpstat** has a number of options that provide different information.

You can obtain a list of your printer requests that are still waiting to print by issuing the **lpstat** command by itself. This will show a list with the ID number of each file queued, your user ID, the size of the file, and the date it was queued.

The option most commonly used with **lpstat** is **-t**, which prints a summary of all status information. Typical output from the **lpstat -t** command for a system that has one printer attached to it (called "laser") would look like this:

```
scheduler is running
system default destination: laser
device for laser: /dev/lp0
laser accepting requests since Aug 10 12:47
printer laser is idle. enabled since Aug 10 12:47
```

This tells us several things. The first line indicates whether the *scheduler* is running. The scheduler works with the print spooler. The print spooler works by creating a temporary file with an image of the print request, and using the scheduler to put them in an order of priority for printing. Then, each file is sent to the printer one at a time. If the scheduler is not running, then the printer must be called directly by the application, instead of invoking the spooler.

The second line in the **lpstat** output indicates the default printer for the system. If no printer is specified when a print request is received, the default printer is used.

The third line indicates the device the default printer is attached to, which, in this case, is the parallel port.

The last two lines tell the user when the printer was last set to accept requests, and when it was enabled. In this case, it was enabled and has accepted requests since August 10th. If the system administrator has to shut the printer down for maintenance, the date for accepting requests may be different but the enabled date will not necessarily change.

The final line also indicates that the printer is idle, and has nothing waiting to be printed. If there are documents waiting to print, **lpstat** lists them with their printer ID numbers. (Remember that each print request is assigned a unique number for tracking through the system.)

The following sample output from the **lpstat -t** command shows that there are two print requests waiting for output, and one currently being printed.

```
scheduler is running
system default destination: laser
device for laser: /dev/lp0
laser accepting requests since Aug 10 12:47
printer laser now printing laser-19. enabled since Aug 10 12:47

laser-19        tim         504     Oct 24 20:17 on laser
laser-20        tim        1643     Oct 24 20:19
laser-21        tim       17625     Oct 24 20:24
```

The listing for each file shows the print ID number, the user who requested the print, the file size in bytes, and the date and time the request was made. As each print request is completed, it is dropped from the list, and the next one is printed.

Cancelling a Print Request (The *cancel* Command)

You can cancel a request you've sent to the printer with the **cancel** command. To cancel a print request, you will need to know the print request number. If it is in the spooler queue, you can find this number with the **lpstat** command. To cancel a print request, issue the command:

```
$cancel IDnumber
```

where "IDnumber" is the print request ID number. These IDs take the form of the name of the printer, a hyphen, and a number. A typical print ID may be "laser-1524".

If the print request you want to cancel is currently printing, you can still cancel it by specifying the name of the printer. Suppose the file is being printed on the printer called "laser". The command:

```
$cancel laser
```

will stop the printing. It is important to note that this will probably not work with printers that have large memories, such as laser printers, as they will have at least part of the file already in the printer RAM, and UNIX cannot control that. As far as UNIX is concerned in these cases, the file has been printed.

Controlling Processes

Everything that is performed on a UNIX system is identified by a unique number called a *process ID* (PID). Every task itself is called a *process*. Some programs are actually several processes executing at once, or in sequence. When you log in to UNIX, the process we call the **login** program runs, and then the process we call the shell starts. Every time you issue a command another process starts.

UNIX uses this system of processes to facilitate multi-tasking. By parcelling every task into a self-contained process, UNIX can readily keep track of what it is doing for each.

Delaying the Start of a Process (The at Command)

UNIX allows you to start a particular process at a later time, even if you will not be logged on. This is useful when you have a time-consuming program to execute and want to set it to proceed when you are not at your terminal, such as during the night. The UNIX **at** command provides this capability.

The format of the **at** command is:

    $at   time day   file

where "time" and "day" are the time and date the instructions in the file "file" are to be executed. The time portion of the command is specified by digits, the first one or two digits interpreted as hours, and the third and fourth as minutes. You do not have to specify the minutes. If you wish to use the twelve-hour time clock, you must specify AM or PM after the digits. If you do not specify AM or PM, UNIX assumes a twenty-four-hour clock.

The "day" in the **at** command is optional: if it is not included, UNIX starts the process at the next time that matches the "time" given in the command. The "day" can be supplied as either the month and day number (such as "11/12" for November 12), or the day of the week (such as "mon").

For example, suppose the file "do_later" contains a series of instructions for executing a task. To start it on the next Monday at 11:00PM, you would issue the **at** command as follows:

```
$at 11pm mon do_later
```

After you enter the command, the UNIX prompt reappears. UNIX waits to execute the "do_later" program until the appointed time, whether you are logged in or not. If the system is rebooted before the task is scheduled to start, though, the command can be lost.

You can determine what programs you have queued at any time by using the **at -l** command. UNIX responds with a list that gives the file name, the user ID, the file's ID number, and the date and time it is due to execute.

To cancel a queued command, you can use **at -r**. The file ID number of the process to be called must be known (from the **at -l** command), as it is used as the argument to **at -r**. The format for **at -r** is:

```
$at file -r ID
```

As a user, you can only remove files you yourself have queued. A superuser can remove any processes. There is another command called *cron* that you can use to start processes at regular times. *Cron* and *at* are discussed again in chapter 10.

Using Background Processing to Do Several Tasks at Once

Suppose you need to run a time consuming program now and also want to do other things on the system at the same time. You can accomplish this by telling UNIX to run the program in background, where you do not see it running. You can have any number of processes running in the background, but only one in the foreground. The *foreground process* is the one you are actively using at the keyboard.

To place a process in the background, use an ampersand (&) after the command. Suppose you have a program that counts a number of entries in a database file, and takes a considerable amount of time to run. Instead of waiting for the program to run on the terminal, you can let it run in the background, and still do other things with the system. If the program was called "runit", you could execute the whole thing in background using the command:

    $runit&

The "runit" program might not execute as quickly in the background as in the foreground, but background processing does allow you to use the terminal while the program is executing.

When a program is running in the background, users cannot interact with it. Therefore, any program that requires someone to type at the keyboard cannot run in the background. If you try to run such a program in the background, when it requires input, it will either stop executing and wait indefinitely for input, or terminate without successfully completing.

A program that writes output to the terminal can run in the background, as long as the output is redirected to a file, or to the *null device* (called "/dev/null"), which disregards all input. It is easier, though, to submit such programs through the **at** command.

Usually, if a background program encounters errors, it terminates by itself, but this does not always happen properly, especially if it is waiting for user input. The best way to stop a background program that is waiting for input is to use the **kill** command.

Killing a Process (The **ps** and **kill** Commands)

You can stop a foreground process at any time during its execution by using the terminal's interrupt key. (This is sometimes the Del key on IBM-PC type keyboards.) This causes UNIX to stop all foreground processing, and return you to the UNIX prompt character.

To stop background processes, you must use the UNIX **kill** command. By itself, **kill** terminates all processes currently running in the background. To stop just one process, you must first determine its identification number (called PID). You can see a full list of all PIDs that belong to you by using the **ps** (processor status) command.

When you type **ps** at the UNIX prompt, UNIX lists the PID, time, and name of each process you are currently executing. A sample **ps** output would look like this:

```
$ps
PID          TTY          TIME          CMD
2435          8f          12:04         -sh
2543          8f          12:20         runit
2567          8f          12:22         ps
```

This example shows three processes currently running under the user's ID. The "TTY" column shows the terminal number the user is logged in at. The "-sh" process is the shell, and is automatically started whenever you log in. The last line shows the "ps" command you were running to get the output.

To kill the "runit" program executing in the background, you would enter the command:

```
$kill 2543
```

This tells UNIX that you wish to terminate the process with a PID of 2543. We will look at *ps* and *kill* again in chapter 10.

Summary

We have looked at several useful UNIX commands for controlling the printer and background tasks in this chapter. They are summarized in Table 4.1. With these commands and the ones you learned in earlier chapters, you should be able to control your use of the printers and background tasks on the system.

Table 4.1: Print and Background Processing Commands

Command	Description
at	delays the start of a process
at -r	removes a process sent **at**
at -q	lists all processes by **at**
cancel	cancels a print request
kill	terminates a process
lp	sends a file to the printer
lpstat	gets printer and spooler status
pr	paginates a file
ps	lists processes executing

Chapter 5

The Mail Program

The UNIX **mail** program provides the ability to send messages and files to other users, even from one system to another. You can also create distribution lists that send the same mail to more than one user.

The **mail** program has been expanded over the years to provide a very powerful system. Instead of covering every possible command and option, we will concentrate here on the aspects of **mail** that will be most useful to you.

Different Versions

There are several versions of the standard UNIX **mail** program included with different versions of UNIX. Most of them are very similar to the standard **mail** discussed in this chapter, but if, for example, a prompt is slightly different or does not appear at all, don't be too concerned. The commands are standard for most of the versions, so there is no need to discuss each minor difference.

The Berkeley release of the standard UNIX **mail** package differs from most others in one important way: It is called **Mail**, with a capital "M". So if you are using BSD UNIX, you will have to remember to type the capital letter whenever this chapter shows the lowercase "m". If you are not sure which version of UNIX you are using, or what your mail system is called, ask your system administrator.

Your Mailbox

Each user has a *mailbox* (a file in which messages are deposited) assigned by the system in the directory "/usr/spool/mail". This is called the *system mailbox*. Also, each user has a *personal mailbox* named "mbox" in their home directory. This one is called the *user mailbox*. When mail is sent to you, it goes to your system mailbox. After you have read it there, you can move it to your user mailbox if you wish to save it. The only way a message can get into your user mailbox is by you moving it there.

Each piece of mail sent between users begins with a common set of information, called the *header*, which lists information about the mail. The header has five parts, as follows:

To:	who the mail is sent to (one or more user names)
Subject:	a description of the message (optional)
CC:	carbon copy user names (optional)
BCC:	blind carbon copy user names (optional)
Receipt:	user names to return receipts to (optional)

Carbon copies are sent as duplicates, and the user names of those receiving copies are listed in the message so you can see who else received a copy. Blind carbon copies are sent to those listed in the BCC field; the message does not mention these recipients. The receipt is an acknowledgement that is issued when a user reads the message.

Mail also includes a *body*, which contains the text of the message.

Each user can have a special file called ".mailrc" in their home directory that contains special instructions for **mail**. This can include identification of mailing lists, changes in commands, and variable settings. If ".mailrc" doesn't exist, **mail** uses default values.

Using Mail: A Quick Example

In order to send a message, you must know the user name of the person to receive the mail. For your first try at using mail, you can send some mail to yourself. At the shell prompt character, enter the command:

    $mail username

Substitute your user name for "username". The mail system will respond with the prompt:

    Subject:

you can enter a brief, one-line description of the message if you wish. Pressing the Return key will complete the entry. If you do not want to enter a description, leave it blank and press Return.

When you have completed the subject description, you are placed in *compose mode* to enter the message you wish to send. The cursor jumps down a line, waiting for you to begin typing the body of the message. For this example, type a few lines of text. While you are in compose mode, pressing Return completes the line you have just typed. A completed line cannot be edited. You can use the backspace key (or the Ctrl-H equivalent) to erase the last character on the current line.

If you want to send carbon copies of the message to other users, you should enter the command:

    ~ c names

on a line by itself. The tilde (~) indicates that you want to exit compose mode temporarily, and issue a command. The tilde is called a *compose escape* for this reason. Compose escapes can be issued at any time while composing mail, and when the command you wished to perform has been completed, you are returned to compose mode.

To specify who should get blind carbon copies, you can enter the command:

    ~ b names

In both commands, "names" represents the user names of the people you wish to cc.

To send the mail you have just composed, press Ctrl-D. When you do this, you get a message from **mail** telling you that your message is completed. Most systems show the prompt:

    (end of message)

and then display the shell prompt character.

Note: BSD UNIX's **Mail** allows you to enter the carbon copy and blind carbon copy information after you have completed the text of the message. To complete your message, type a period on a line by itself and press Return. You are then prompted for the copy-routing information.

To read the mail you just sent to yourself, you can enter the mail system without providing a user name:

    $mail

This tells **mail** to display the headers, in an abbreviated form, of any messages that are waiting for you. In this example, there is one message waiting—the one you just sent.

    mail version 3.0 January 28, 1987. Type ? for help
    1 message:
    1 tim   Tue Jul 11 13:07   8/192   "test"

The **mail** system then puts you in another mode called *command mode*. This is indicated by the underscore character in the left margin.

If you have nothing waiting in your mailbox, **mail** displays "no messages" and then redisplays the shell prompt character.

If you have mail, pressing the Return key displays the first message that is waiting for you. If you have more than one piece of mail, pressing Return again displays the next piece, and so on. After you have read your messages, you can quit the **mail** program by entering **q**.

Sending Mail

As you have just seen, you can send mail to users by specifying their names after the **mail** command. The command:

    `$mail joe bill tom`

places you in compose mode. When you press Ctrl-D after typing your message, your message is sent to all three named users.

You may also want to send a file that was not created in compose mode. You can use UNIX's redirection capabilities to send this type of mail. For example, suppose you have used a word processor or editor to create a document called "letter". You can send it to another user with the command:

    `$mail username < letter`

where "username" is the user you wish to send the file "letter" to.

More than one person can receive the file. The command:

    `$mail bill tim  bob  < letter`

sends the file "letter" to the three users "bill", "tim", and "bob".

You can send any kind of file using **mail**, including spreadsheet information, statistical data, or even graphics. The **mail** program doesn't actually "read" or try to understand the file, so it doesn't care what the contents are.

Mail can be edited from within **mail**, by using the **e** command (to invoke **ed**) or the **v** command (to invoke **vi**). The mail is copied to a temporary file, then the editor is called. When you finish with the editor, the mail is copied back in to **mail**.

Reading Mail

As you have seen, when you want to see if you have received any messages, you enter the **mail** command by itself at the shell prompt character. When you do this, the program checks your system mailbox, and displays the headers of any messages you have received. If your messages require more than one screen, you can scroll the pages with the **h+** or **h-** commands (header forward and back). Mail is displayed in reverse chronological order, the most recently received mail is listed and displayed first.

When you are in the **mail** program, you can scan the mail from a particular user with the command:

    h username

"Username" is the user's logon name. The subject headers of all mail from this user are displayed.

The list of headers tells you what actions have been performed on the various messages. Any deleted messages do not appear, of course. If a command has an **M** next to it, it will be saved in your personal mailbox when you leave **mail**. An asterisk next to the mail indicates that it will be saved (using the **save** command). If any mail option for holding messages is set, an **H** may appear, indicating that a particular message is being held. Don't be too worried about what these mean—we will see them again shortly!

When you exit the **mail** system using the **q** command, all mail marked for deletion is permanently removed. If you have marked any mail for saving in your personal mailbox, it is moved over. If you wish to exit **mail** quickly without deleting or saving the mail, you can do so with the **x** command. This allows you to leave **mail** without the normal housekeeping functions.

To read the most recent mail, press the Return key. You can read messages by entering their numbers. You can move along the list of messages by using the **+n** and **-n** commands, where "n" is the number of messages to skip. To display a specific message, you can use the **p** (print) command with the message's number. For example, if your list of messages is:

            3 tim   Tue Jul 11 13:07   8/192   "test"
            2 bill   Mon Jul 10 09:52   6/83   "meeting tomorrow"
            1 mary   Sun Jul 9 15:23   6/83   "Useful Info"

you can specify that you want to see only the second message with the command:

    p 2

at which point **mail** will display only that message. Note that p(print) refers to the screen, not to the printer. After reading the second message, if you wanted to read the third, you could enter - or **-1** to move up a message and display that one. To read the next message you can enter **+** or just press Return. All movement commands are relative to the last message read. If you are not sure which message you are currently positioned at, you can enter the command **=**, and **mail** will respond with the message number.

Another method of scanning your mail is to use the **top** command. This displays the first five lines of the messages in your mailbox. The command:

    top 1-3

displays the first five lines of your first three messages. The number of lines that **top** displays can be set in your ".mailrc" file.

If you would like a hard copy of a message, you can send it to the printer with the l command and an argument telling **mail** which message to send. For example, the command:

    l 3

prints out the third message, whereas:

    l tim

prints all messages received from "tim". The printouts are paginated automatically.

Saving Your Mail (The **mb** and **s** Commands)

To save the displayed mail in your user mailbox, use the **mb** command. When you exit **mail**, all items you have marked for saving in this way will be placed in your user mailbox, and deleted from your system mailbox. Instead of saving the mail in your user mailbox, you can also redirect it to a file by giving a file name after the **s** (save) command. For example, typing:

```
s fromjoe
```

saves the currently displayed mail in a file called "fromjoe" in the current directory. It is deleted from your system mailbox after the file has been completed.

If new mail should arrive for you while you are in the mail program, a message appears at the bottom of the screen:

```
New mail has arrived--type 'restart' to read.
```

Typing **restart** forces the program to check your mailbox again and display the new headers.

If you want to access your user mailbox instead of your system mailbox, you must tell **mail** what file to use. Your user mailbox is called "mbox" and is kept in your home directory, so to use this as the mailbox for **mail** to work with, give the command:

```
$mail -f mbox
```

at the shell prompt character. The **-f** option tells **mail** to use the specified file as the mailbox file. If you don't specify a file name in this way, **mail** assumes you want the system mailbox.

Deleting, Undeleting, Replying, and Forwarding Mail

Deleting and Undeleting

You can delete mail after you have read it by typing **d** (delete) at the prompt. This removes the message from the header list, but you can recall deleted mail with the **u** (undelete) command, as long as you are still in the same **mail** session. You can delete all your mail with one command, using a wildcard:

```
d *
```

This erases all your mail from you mailbox. You can also delete a range of messages. For example, the command:

    d 1-8

deletes your first eight messages.

A quick way to read through your mailbox is to use the command **dp**, which deletes the current message, and displays the next one.

The **u** command uses a number as an argument to tell it which message to undelete:

    u number

"Number" is the mail identification number.

Replying to a Mail Message

After reading a message, you can reply to it by using the **r** (reply) command. When you enter the reply command, you are placed in compose mode, and can create a message as if you were starting a new piece of mail. When you press Ctrl-D, the reply is sent automatically to the user who sent you the message you are replying to. (The routing information is retained by **mail**, so you do not have to reenter it.)

If you reply by using the uppercase **R** command, **mail** asks for the user names of other users you may wish to send the message to, either directly or as a carbon copy.

Forwarding a Mail Message

You can forward messages to other users by using the **f** command with the user name as an argument. For example, the command:

    f bill

forwards the last displayed message to user "bill". The subject or header is modified to indicate that the message was forwarded from you. The entire text of the message is shifted to the right one tab stop. If you do not want the text of the copy shifted, use the uppercase **F** command, which is otherwise identical to the lowercase command. Using uppercase **F** can make the forwarded message appear neater and easier to read.

To forward mail to more than one user, include the names of all the users or use a distribution list (see the following section). You can forward a specific message if you supply its number, otherwise **mail** assumes you want to forward the most recently displayed message. The command:

```
f 5 tim bill bob
```

forwards message number 5 to the three users named.

Saving Time with Mailing Lists (The **alias** Command)

A *mailing list,* also known as an *alias* or *distribution list,* allows you to send messages to several people at once without having to type their names every time. You create a mailing list by specifying the users who belong to a particular group with the **alias** command.

Mailing lists are defined by adding to the ".mailrc" file in your home directory. The following sample command assigns the group name "programmers" to the four users specified:

```
alias programmers tim bill bob mary
```

Now if you send a message to "programmers", each of the four will get a copy. Additionally, when a reply is sent *from* a mailing list, all the people on the mailing list get a copy, unless this feature is overridden.

An alias can be set inside **mail** using either **alias** or its short form, **a**. For example, issuing either the command:

```
a sales deb mary sue john
```

or its expanded version:

```
alias sales deb mary sue john
```

assigns the distribution list "sales" to the four users. Any aliases defined inside **mail** are lost when you exit **mail**. To be accessible at all times, they must be saved in your **.mailrc** file. The **.mailrc** file is created and saved with an editor or work processor.

The system administrator can set system-wide aliases, which can be used by all users. Otherwise, all aliases defined in your **.mailrc** file are for your personal use.

The .mailrc File

The ".mailrc" file is a file in which you can store customized settings for your use of the **mail** program. Usually you have to create a .mailrc file for yourself. This can be done with an editor, such as **ed** or **vi**, or by **cat**ting to a file. ".mailrc" files often contain only distribution list definitions, such as:

```
alias programmers tim bill bob mary
alias analysts john simon deb sue jenny kim
alias sales mary alex david
```

All such settings work only for your login.

Summary of Mail Commands

You can see a help screen summary of all **mail** commands by entering ? or **help** at the **mail** prompt. (This does not work in compose mode unless you type a tilde (~) first. Recall that the tilde is a "compose escape", which tells **mail** the next character is a command rather than a character in the mail message text.) Some versions of **mail** use the asterisk (*) as the help character, so if you don't get the help screen using a question mark, try an asterisk.

The **mail** program uses simple commands throughout. The basic commands are listed in Table 5.1.

Table 5.1: Mail's Basic Commands

Command	Description
a	creates an alias (distribution list)
~b	adds names to the blind carbon copy list
~c	adds names to the carbon copy list
d	deletes displayed or specified (with a numeric argument) messages
dp	deletes displayed message and displays the next one
e	invokes editor
h	scrolls headers forward or back
f	forwards mail to another user
F	forwards mail without shifting text to the right
l	prints a hard copy
mb	saves message in your personal mailbox
n	skips n pieces of mail (+/-)
p	displays (print) mail
q	quits with cleanup of mailbox
r	replies to mail
R	replies to multiple users
restart	restarts mail and check for new messages
s	saves to a file
top	displays first five lines of specified messages
u	undeletes (restores) deleted mail
v	invokes **vi**
x	quits with no cleanup of mailbox
?	displays help screen summary
=	displays current message number
!	invokes a shell command without leaving mail

Chapter 6

Using the Editors ed and vi

The basic UNIX editor, **ed**, is limited in its capabilities, so most UNIX implementations offer a more powerful editor called **vi**. If **vi** is available on your system, you may want to skip the section on **ed** and move straight on to **vi**.

Most users will find themselves using **ed** infrequently, especially if **vi** or another editor is available. However, as an emergency editor, it functions well, and its commands are not difficult to learn. You will find the same commands used in many UNIX programs, such as **vi**, **mail**, and others.

A Little About Editors

All editors perform the same basic operations. To know how UNIX editors work, you must understand how they use editing buffers. An editing buffer is a temporary file that the editor creates for you when you run it. Any text you type or changes you make are initially recorded in this buffer. Until you tell the editor to write the contents of the buffer to the original file, these changes can all be lost or aborted.

This has an advantage if you are modifying an existing file. If, by accident, you make some deletions or alter the file in some way that you wish you hadn't, you can quit the editor without saving the contents of the editing buffer, and your original file will be in the same condition it was in when you started. On the other hand, if you forget to save your work, several hours can be lost in a fraction of a second!

Most editors have two types or *modes* of operation: *command mode* and *text mode*. Command mode waits for you to tell the editor what to do; each character you type is assumed to be an instruction to the editor, and not part of the file you are working on. Text mode (also called *compose mode*) assumes that whatever you type is part of the file and not a command. To issue a command when in text mode, you must first use a special character called a *compose escape*. (Recall that we discussed escaping from compose mode in the chapter on using **mail**.)

Editors fall into two categories. A line editor manipulates text on a line-by-line basis, and it requires you to indicate what line you want a command to act on. Line editors were originally developed for use with paper printout terminals, for which full screen operation was impossible, and for slow terminals for which full screen operation was awkward.

A screen editor, as its name implies, works with a full screen at a time. It is display-oriented, and allows you to move about a file by using cursor keys. Any changes you make to a file are shown immediately on the display.

UNIX's built-in line editor is **ed**, while **vi** is the screen editor supplied with most UNIX versions. They each have advantages and disadvantages, depending on the hardware you are working on, although **vi** is very quickly becoming the standard editor.

Using **ed**

A quick editing session with **ed** will give you an idea of what it can do, and acquaint you with some of the basic editing commands. You can invoke the editor by typing **ed** at the shell prompt:

```
$ ed
```

The cursor drops down a line, and waits for you to type commands. The file you are currently working on is kept as a temporary file that will be saved under a different name later. The temporary file is referred to as the **editing buffer**. If you wish to supply a filename when you invoke the editor, you can provide it as an argument to the **ed** command:

    $ed filename

where "filename" is the name of the file.

Entering Text with ed (The *a*, *p*, *w*, and *q* Commands)

Now, you can use the **a** command (for add) to add text. When you enter the **a** command, the cursor jumps down a line, and you can enter text. Pressing the Return key separates lines, as usual. Enter:

    a

Now press Return, and then type:

    Line 1 of 5
    line 2 of 5
    Line 3 of 5
    line 4 of 5
    Line 5 of 5

Text addition is completed with Ctrl-D, or a period on a line by itself. If you typed the five lines above and then pressed Ctrl-D, your editing buffer now contains five lines. You may find that Ctrl-D doesn't take you out of compose mode. This will be because you are part way through a line. Ctrl-D must be on a line by itself to exit from compose mode.

Each line you enter is assigned a line number by **ed**. All references to the text are by line numbers. If you want to find out what the current line number is, just enter an equal sign on a line by itself.

You can display text in the editing buffer with the **p** command, preceded by the lines to be displayed. The command:

    1,5p

displays lines one through five of the editing buffer. The command:

    3p

displays the third line. The command **p** by itself displays the line the editor is currently aligned with. If you use invalid line numbers, **ed** responds with a question mark, indicating it doesn't understand the command.

Text added with the **a** command is always appended to the end of the file.

You save the text with the **w** command. If you have not yet specified a filename, you must specify one now. Type:

    w filename

where "filename" is the name of the file. When you give this command, **ed** responds with a message that indicates the number of characters that have been saved. If you are writing a large file, it is a good practice to save the information frequently by issuing the **w** command at regular intervals.

You quit the editor with the **q** command. If you supplied a filename when you started **ed**, the **q** command exits the program directly. If the buffer has not been written to a file with the **w** command, **ed** respond with a question mark to indicate that the text will be lost. If you want to save the buffer, enter **w** before enter **q** again. To exit without saving the work, just enter another **q**.

Reading in an Existing File (The e and r Commands)

To read an existing file into the editing buffer, **ed** uses the **e** command (for edit):

    e filename

where "filename" is the name of the file to be read into the buffer. When **ed** reads the file in, it displays a message that indicates the number of characters that are in the file.

When a file has been read in using the **e** command, **ed** will use this filename as the default when you issue a **w** command to write any changes. Therefore, if you start editing a file called "temp1", then read in "temp2" and issue the **w** command, it is "temp2" that is updated, not "temp1". To force the saved information to another file, you must explicitly indicated the filename with the **w** command:

    w temp1

This saves the file as "temp1".

The **e** command overwrites any information currently in the editing buffer. If you write ten lines, then issue the **e** command, the existing ten lines are destroyed and replaced by the incoming file.

If you do not want to overwrite what is currently in the editing buffer, use the **r** command (for read) instead of **e**. This places the text of the specified file at the end of the current editing buffer, without damaging the existing contents of the buffer. Like the **e** command, the **r** command responds with the number of characters it has read in.

Getting to Know ed

Occasionally, you may forget the name of the file you are working on. You can recall the name with the **f** command. **ed** responds with the default filename. You can change the name with the **f** command also. Entering:

    f newname

where "newname" is the new default filename, sets that file as the one that is saved when you issue a **w**.

The **f** command has a useful trick associated with it. Suppose you want to read in and edit a file called "file1", but want to preserve it as it is. After calling in "file1" with the **e** command, or as an argument to the **ed** shell command, you can issue the command:

    f file2

and all changes you make in the editor will be saved as "file2".

We have already looked briefly at the **p** (for print) command, and have seen that we can display certain lines or a range of lines by specifying their line numbers. Sometimes we don't know the number of lines in the buffer, though, so we can use an **ed** shorthand symbol to indicate the last line of the text. The command:

```
1,$p
```

prints all lines from the first to the last. When you are specifying line numbers, the dollar sign always means the last line of the editing buffer.

Simple math functions can be combined in commands. For example, you can use both addition and subtraction from a specified line number can be used. To print out the last five lines of the file (assuming there are five or more lines), for instance, you might use the command:

```
$-5,$p
```

The current line is indicated by the shorthand symbol of the period. To print the next two lines from the current line, use the command:

```
.,.+2p
```

You can print the file from the current position to the end by issuing the command:

```
.,$p
```

You can always display a single line by using the line number, but **ed** has a shorthand form for this too. Instead of specifying "6p", for example, simply entering "6" accomplishes the same task. The editor assumes when you enter a line number by itself that you want to move to that line and display it. In a similar manner, it is not even necessary to specify the plus sign for lines in a range. If a sign is not indicated, **ed** assumes you mean to add to it. Therefore, the commands:

```
.,.+4p
```

and

      .,.4p

mean the same to **ed**.

You can step through a file a line at a time in either direction by using the plus and minus signs by themselves. If you are at line 6, for example, and issue the plus sign, **ed** moves you down to line seven, and displays that line. The minus sign moves you back one, and displays the contents of that line.

Continuing with **ed**'s trend to abbreviate commands you can increase or decrease, the plus and minus movement through text is with either numbers or signs. The command "++", for example, moves down two lines, as does "+2".

All of these commands can sometimes lead to confusion as to exactly what line you are actually on! You can always determine this, however, by entering the equal sign. The editor will return a message with the current line number.

Deleting, Inserting, Changing and Moving Lines (The **d**, **i**, **c**, and **m** Commands)

The *delete* command is the letter **d**, and is used in exactly the same manner as the **p** command. Line ranges, single lines, or shorthand notations all work with **d**. The command:

      2,5d

for example, deletes lines two through five, inclusive. The line numbers that remain are all renumbered in sequence. The current line number is reset to the end of the file.

You can *insert* lines with the **i** command. Lines are always inserted *before* the current line, so take care to move past the line that is to be followed by inserted text before entering **i**. You can use the insert command with the search command, to look for a line:

/string/i

which will insert a line before the line that contains the characters "string". We will look at the search commands in a moment.

Lines can also be changed directly, instead of deleting the old ones and inserting new ones. When you give the **c** command, **ed** uses the lines you then type at the terminal to replace the same number of lines in the text. You can specify the lines to be changed, by entering their range, as you do with the **p** command. For example, the command:

1,5c

replaces the first five lines of the text with whatever is typed at the keyboard.

Moving text is accomplished with the **m** command. You specify the line, or range of lines, to be moved, as well as the target line number. For example, the command:

1,5m$

moves lines one through five to the end of the file (indicated by the "$"), and renumbers the lines. Lines that are moved are placed *after* the specified target line number.

As with most **ed** commands, shortforms are allowed, and these can be used for quick text manipulation. The command:

m+

transposes the current line with the line following it.

Searching for Text (The / and ? Commands)

Locating a specific string of characters inside a file is tedious if each line must be examined visually. The **ed** program provides a search capability, which is much like the search command we used with the **more** program earlier. The format of the command is:

/string/

where "string" represents the characters to be located. The last slash character can be omitted.

The search occurs from the current line down to the end of the text. If **ed** finds the string, it prints the line. If it does not find the string, it responds with the message:

>   ?
>   search string not found

and positions itself at the end of the text. You can force **ed** to "wrap" the search around from the end to the start again, and then search through to the current line by entering:

>   .+1,./string/

This tells **ed** to search to the end, then go to line number 1 and search to the "dot line" or current line.

Sometimes, you know the string you want to find is above the current line. You can instruct **ed** to search backwards through the text by using question marks instead of slashes:

>   /string/   searches forward
>   ?string?   searches backward

When you have located the first occurrence of a string, you can search for the same string again using the simple command:

>   //

This instructs **ed** to search for the last string given. To search again backwards, use the command:

>   ??

You can use these commands as many times as required to locate the desired occurrences of the string.

Replacing Text (The s, g, v, and u Commands)

Editing existing text is a necessary function for most users. The **ed** *substitute* command, **s**, is used to perform most editing functions. This allows you to modify a single line at a time. If the current line reads:

```
UNIX is a grate operating symtem.
```

and you want to change "grate" to "great", you must use the **s** command format:

```
#s/oldstring/newstring
```

where "#" is the line number, "oldstring" is the string to be replaced, and "newstring" is the replacing string. Thus, the command to change "grate" to "great" in the line above (assuming it is line number 7) would be:

```
7s/grate/great
```

To look at the new line you can issue the **p** command. The editor allows the **p** command to be appended to most commands, including **s**, so that the line can be immediately examined after a substitution. If the above command is written:

```
7s/grate/great/p
```

the line is printed after the substitution. (Only the **p** command can be appended in this way with **ed**.)

If you were currently positioned on line 7, you could let **ed** assume that you wanted the current line without explicitly stating so. The command then is:

```
s/grate/great
```

Similarly, to correct the spelling of "system" in the same line, any command that accomplishes the required change can be used. Several commands can perform the same function in this case. Typing any of the following:

```
7s/symtem/system
7s/sym/sys
7s/ym/ys
```

all result in the correction. Generally, the identifying string has to be long enough to ensure that only the single correction we want to make is performed, without affecting other parts of the string by accident.

You can specify the line numbers to be replaced as a range, if required, as in the command:

    1,$s/UNYX/UNIX

This would replace all occurrences of "UNYX" with "UNIX" throughout the text.

You can also use the substitution command to eliminate letters or words, by replacing them with a null (empty) string:

    p
    This is the 10thxxx line
    s/xxx//p
    This is the 10th line

Note that there can be no space between the two slashes, or **ed** would insert a space.

The substitution command format as we have used it so far will only replace the first occurrence of the replacement string. If a string occurs in more than one location in a line, the format must be modified slightly. The string **/g** is appended (for global) to the **s** command to indicate that all occurrences are to be replaced on each line specified in the range.

The global flag **g** can also be used with other commands. For example, to print all lines that contain the string "UNIX", you would use the command:

    g/UNIX/p

An opposite form of the **g** command is the **v** option, which specifies those lines that do not match the criteria. Therefore, the command:

    v/UNIX/p

would print all those lines that do not have the string "UNIX" in them.

The two commands **g** and **v** can be used with any valid **ed** command. For example, the command:

    g/UNIX/d

deletes all lines containing the string "UNIX".

You can combine the search and replace commands on the same command line, if desired. For example, the command:

    /UNYX/s/UNYX/UNIX/p

searches forward for the string "UNYX", and when it locates it, replaces it with "UNIX", then prints the newly corrected line.

Combinations of commands extend beyond search and replace. The command:

    g/UNYX/s//UNIX/gp

for example, globally changes all occurrences of the "UNYX" string with "UNIX" and prints the results. The command causes a global search for "UNYX", then, when it is encountered, replaces it with "UNIX". The double slashes "//" tell the command to repeat the previous search (for "UNYX") when executing the global instruction, while the trailing "/g" ensures we get all those conditions where "UNYX" may occur more than once on a single line.

If you have performed a substitution, and realize it was done in error, **ed** allows you to "undo" it, by using the **u** command. The **u** function restores a line to its previous state before substitution occurred. The undo feature only applies to the substitution command, and does not work with global replacements. **ed** has more commands than we have seen here, but you now have the basis you need to use **ed** to edit and save your files. For more details on **ed**, you can consult the user's guides that came with your UNIX system. Ask your system administrator if you want more information.

The **vi** Editor

Many UNIX implementations have a powerful editor called **vi** (for "visual editor"), which is screen oriented. The **vi** editor is much more powerful than **ed**, and can be used as a programmer's editor. Unless a third party word processor or programmer editor is added to the UNIX system, it is most likely you will work with **vi**.

The **vi** editor has a lot of power, and it is best to begin by learning the basics, then expand your capabilities with the editor as you need them. There may be a lot to learn, but don't be overwhelmed. Most of the **vi** commands are easy to learn: it is the complex "tricks" you can do with these commands that take a little more time to master.

Creating and Exiting a File

To create a document, use the name of the file as an argument to the command **vi**:

```
$vi testfile
```

The screen clears and a row of tildes (~) appears down the left side. At the bottom the name of the file is shown. Notice that you are working with a full screen of information, instead of the line by line orientation imposed by **ed**.

The tildes on the screen do not show real lines in the text, yet, as we haven't actually put anything in. Instead, they show the screen lines only. They have no meaning when we save the file. The cursor is at the top of the screen. The line the cursor is on is called the *current line*.

Start by entering text. To do this, first enter *insert mode*, using the **i** command. Then, type three or four lines of text. Pressing the Return key saves each line as it is typed. When you have finished entering some text, exit insert mode by pressing the ESC key. This places you in *command mode*.

The bottom line of the screen usually shows the name of the file, and either "New File" or "Modified" in square brackets, depending on whether you have called up an existing file.

While in command mode, press Ctrl-G. You will notice that the bottom line of the screen now displays more information about your file. The status line appears when you are searching for characters, when error messages must be displayed, and when some other commands are executed. You can always see the command line by Ctrl-G. A typical **vi** status line looks like this:

```
"myfile" [Modified]   line 10 of 100   --10%--
```

It tells you the name of the file you are currently editing, whether the file has been modified since it was last saved, the current line number and the total number of lines in the file, as well as the cursor location as a percentage of the file. The status line disappears as you use **vi**, but it can always be recalled in command mode.

You can read an existing file into the current file using the **r** command. This command expects a colon before the command and the filename after the command:

```
:r filename
```

where "filename" is the file to be read into the existing file. You must be in command mode to use this command. The colon is a special instruction to **vi**, which you will learn about shortly.

Leaving **vi** requires you to drop to command mode, if you are not already in it, by using the Esc key. To save the current file and exit to the shell, the command is:

```
:x
```

Note again that the colon is necessary.

To quit without saving the file you are working on, use the command:

```
:q!
```

Any changes made to the file during this session are not saved.

You may want to save your current file *without* exiting to the shell. To do this, use the command:

    :w

The default filename is assumed unless another is specified.

Moving Around the Screen

The **vi** editor lets you use the full screen for editing, so it is not surprising that it provides a way to move around the screen. Naturally, the cursor arrow keys can control the cursor position. But so can another set of keys:

    h   left
    j   down
    k   up
    l   right

These keys were chosen because they are close to each other on the keyboard. Because they are not intuitively obvious, using these keys does require a bit of practice. (These keys also are used in other UNIX programs, so it is worthwhile learning what they do now.) You can only move the cursor in command mode. If you are inserting text, they will not move you about in the same way.

The cursor movement keys can also be used to move around the file in large jumps. Other movement commands are used with **vi**, but you may not find all of them useful. The full list of movement keys is given in table 3.2.

You can move to a specific line with the **G** command. If you enter "5G", for example, the cursor goes to the start of the fifth line. (If you did not have five lines in the file, the cursor would not move.)

Simple Editing with **vi**

The **vi** editor has a number of commands that you will find quite useful. One of the most frequently used commands is the "repeat" command, which repeats the most recent insert or delete command. For example, if you have just entered three lines of text in insert mode, you can repeat those lines by typing a period. Say you had originally typed:

```
This is a test.
This is only a test.
Do not be alarmed!
```

then you issue the repeat command by typing a period alone, your text now appears as:

```
This is a test.
This is only a test.
Do not be alarmed!
This is a test.
This is only a test.
Do not be alarmed!
```

The repeat command always executes below the current line (the line containing the cursor).

You have just duplicated a block of text, so now you can get rid of it with the undo command, **u**. This command restores the text to the state it was in prior to the last command. If you issued the **u** command after performing the repeat above, you would have your original three lines back. If you issued it again, the removal of the three lines would be undone, and you would have all six lines again! The undo command is very useful for recovering from accidental deletions.

You have already used the **i** command to insert text, but sometimes you may wish to change a file's contents by *overwriting* the existing text. You can do this with the **r** (for replace) command. The replace command has two formats. The first simply replaces the letter the cursor is on with a specified letter. For example, the command:

```
rX
```

replaces the current character with the character "X". Repeats are also supported, so the command:

```
10rX
```

replaces ten characters with "X"s. To move into a *replace mode*, use the **R** command. In this mode, you replace text until **vi** receives an ESC. The uppercase **R** put you in replace mode, while the lowercase **r** does not. **r** replaces only specified letters. To leave replace mode, the Esc key is used.

To delete lines, use the **d** command. You can use the delete command to specify which lines to delete, or use it in conjunction with the cursor movement keys to specify variations in the delete function. The supported delete commands are summarized in Table 3.3.

You can delete characters from the cursor position either to the right, or to the left. The command for deletion to the right is **x**, while the command to delete to the left is **X**. A number indicates a repeated delete. For example, the command:

    5x

deletes the character the cursor is on and the next four to the right, while the command:

    10X

deletes the ten characters immediately preceding the cursor.

Words are deleted with the **dw** command. Issuing the command:

    5dw

deletes the five words, including the word the cursor is on, to the right of the cursor.

Lines are deleted with the **dd** command. If a line number is given, that particular line is deleted. For example, the command:

    5dd

deletes line 5.

The delete commands can also be used to delete a range of lines. The command:

    :50,100d

deletes lines 50 to 100, inclusive. The status line displays a message telling you that 50 lines were involved in the deletion. The command:

    :.,+10d

deletes the current line and the next 10 lines. To delete lines preceding the current line, you would use the minus sign with the number of lines to be removed. You may have noticed we used a color in front of the last two commands. They are required to make **vi** function properly. The color indicates to **vi** that the commands are line oriented, instead of screen oriented.

The **vi** editor allows you to temporarily suspend work on the file you are in, to execute other UNIX commands. This is called a *shell escape*, because you are escaping from your current work to access the shell. You should specify the command you wish to execute as part of the escape command format, as in the following:

    :!lc

where "lc" is the command you wish to run. The colon and exclamation mark identify the shell escape characters for **vi**. When you execute a shell command, **vi** prompts you to press Return to continue with your **vi** session.

To determine which line you are currently on in a file, you can use the Ctrl-G sequence we saw earlier, or use the command:

    :nu

This shows the line number and the text of the current line on the status line at the bottom of the screen. Most line-oriented commands require you to know where you are in the file, so this command is useful.

Searching and Replacing Text

Searching for words with **vi** uses the same basic command structure as the **more** program we used earlier, as well as that of **ed**. A search string is identified with a slash character, followed by the string to be located. The search occurs from the current cursor position to the end of the text, then wraps around to the beginning. To search for the word "foobar" in the file, you would use the command:

    `/foobar`

When a match is found, the cursor is placed on the matching string. The next occurrence of the string can be found by entering the letter **n** (for next).

Backward searches use the question mark instead of the slash character. The command:

    `?foobar`

searches for "foobar" from the cursor back through the file to the top.

You can match sets of characters with the search function by enclosing valid characters in square brackets. For example, the command:

    `/[Ff]oobar`

matches either "Foobar" or "foobar". Ranges of characters and numbers are treated as ASCII values, enabling the command:

    `/[a-z]oobar`

to match "aoobar" through "zoobar".

Replacing text automatically requires that **vi** change from screen-oriented mode to line-oriented. The difference between the two is that screen-oriented works on the whole screen from the cursor location on, while line-oriented commands must specify where the task is to be performed. Line-oriented commands are all preceded by a colon.

The format of the search and replace command is:

    `:1,$s/oldstring/newstring/g`

where the "1,$" tells **vi** to search from the first line to the end of the document (symbolized by the dollar sign), and replace all occurrences of "oldstring" with "newstring". The trailing **/g** tells **vi** that all occurrences on a single line are to be converted. If this had been left off, only the first occurrence of "oldstring" on each line would be changed.

The case of the strings is significant, so it may be necessary to perform multiple search and replace operations if the string to be converted could occur with different capitalizations. The entire search and replace operation can be revoked with the **u** (undo) command.

Copying and Moving Lines

There are two ways of copying lines from one part of the file to another. The first involves a direct copy command, while the second uses a buffer to store the text.

You can copy lines from one part of the file to another using the **co** command. To illustrate the use of **co**, try copying lines 10 through 20 from a file, and placing them after line 5 with the command:

    :10,20 co 5

From this example, you can see the format. You specify the lines to be copied first, then the target line, after the **co** command. The copied lines are inserted after the target line.

If you are not sure where you want to insert the lines, or want to copy several lines to more than one location, the **vi** *buffer* provides an easier way to do this. First, you move to the line you want to copy, then, to copy this line into the **vi** buffer, you issue the command:

    "ayy

which "yanks" the line into the buffer called "a". Now, you can move to another part of the document, and put the line in there. The command:

    "ap

"puts" the contents of buffer "a" in at the cursor line. The "a" buffer still contains a copy of the line you "yanked", despite the fact that you have "put" it somewhere. Thus, we could repeat the "put" command many times, after copying it into the buffer only once.

You can "yank" any number of lines into the buffer by specifying the number of lines desired. The command:

    `"a5yy`

"yanks" the next five lines into buffer "a".

In a similar fashion, you can "yank" words instead of lines. The command to copy words into the buffer is similar to that for lines. The command:

    `"a5yw`

"yanks" the next five words, including the word the cursor is on, into the buffer "a". You can "yank" characters, too. The command:

    `"a10yl`

"yanks" the next ten characters ("l" is the cursor right character). The cursor movement commands are valid with the copy to a buffer, so that the command:

    `"ay$`

copies from the current cursor position to the end of the line.

Moving text works the same way as copying. The command:

    `:5m10`

moves line 5 to the position after line 10. You can also specify ranges to move. For example, the command:

    `:5,10m20`

moves lines 5 through 10 to the position after line 20.

Buffers can be used to move text, but the operation is different than with the copy command. Instead of *copying* text into a buffer, you *delete* it into the buffer. The **vi** editor maintains nine delete buffers, which are labeled 1 through 9. Buffer 1 always contains the most recent deletion. When more text is deleted, buffer 1 gets bumped to buffer 2, and the newly deleted text gets put in buffer 1, and so on, as more text gets deleted. When text is "bumped" out of buffer 9, it is lost.

Moving text using the buffers means deleting it, then recalling it from a delete buffer. Suppose you want to move a single line of text elsewhere in the document. You first position yourself on the line to be moved and issue the line delete command:

    dd

Then you move the cursor to the line the text is to be moved to and issue the command:

    "1p

This recalls the contents of delete buffer 1 and places it at the cursor line. As with the copy buffers, putting text into the file from the delete buffers does not remove the contents of the buffer, so any buffer can be "put" a number of times.

If you were going to move three lines, you would move the cursor to the three different lines, and line delete each one. The contents of the three lines would now reside in buffers 1 through 3. Each could be recalled with the "put" command, using the different buffer numbers.

Summary of Editor Commands

Tables 6.1 through 6.3 summarize the commands you have learned in this chapter for using the UNIX editors, **ed** and **vi**.

The **vi** editor offers a lot of commands that allow experienced users to work more efficiently. We have not been able to cover all of **vi**'s capabilities in this book, but some of the more useful "tricks" can be found in advanced UNIX books.

Table 6.1: Summary of *ed* Commands

Command	Description
a	adds or appends text to the end of the file
c	changes lines
d	deletes text
e	reads text from another file (overwrites current contents)
f	displays or changes current working filename
i	inserts lines before the current line
p	prints lines from the buffer
r	reads text from another file (doesn't overwrite contents)
u	undoes last substitution command
w	writes the buffer to a file
q	quits the editor
=	displays current line number
+	displays next line
-	displays previous line
.	quits text mode and enters command mode

Table 6.2: The *vi* Cursor Movement Commands

Command	Description
b	back one word
h	left one character
j	down one line
k	up one line
l	right one character
w	forward one word
0	beginning of current line
$	end of current line
G	goes to a specific line
H	top left corner of screen
L	lowest line on screen
Ctrl-U	scrolls up 1/2 screen
Ctrl-D	scrolls down 1/2 screen
Ctrl-F	scrolls down 1 screen
Ctrl-B	scrolls up 1 screen

Table 6.3: The vi Delete Commands

Command	Description
dd	deletes current line
dw	deletes from cursor to end of word
x	deletes character cursor is on
d$	deletes from cursor to end of line
D	deletes from cursor to end of line
d0	deletes from cursor to start of line

Chapter 7

Completing the Fundamentals

You used several UNIX commands in earlier chapters to create, move, and delete files. UNIX also has a very large set of utility programs that you can use for a wide variety of tasks. In this chapter, you will learn some of the more useful ones.

Finding a File (The **find** Comment)

When you are working with several subdirectories, it is easy to forget exactly where you saved a particular file. You may remember the name, or part of it, but not the directory. The UNIX **find** command offers a wide variety of search capabilities. However, because the **find** command is so powerful, it is also a little awkward to use until you gain some familiarity with it.

The **find** command has a lengthy list of arguments, but to begin, you can use it in a very basic form. If you know a file's name and want to determine its directory location, the **find** command's syntax is:

```
find pathname -name file name -print
```

where "pathname" is the directory or directory tree to be searched, and "file name" is the file to be located. The directory specified with the **find** command is searched *recursively*, that is, the **find** command searches the named directory and then searches all directories underneath it.

The "-name" option indicates that you are going to specify the file name to search for. The "-print" option tells **find** to direct the output of the command to the terminal.

If you want to locate a file called "foobar", for example, which is in the directory "/usr/tim" or one of its subdirectories, for example, the command is:

    $find /usr/tim -name foobar -print

This results in a list of all matching names, printed at the terminal. A typical output might look like this:

    /usr/tim/foobar
    /usr/tim/notes/foobar
    /usr/tim/book/draft/foobar

Each line gives the full directory and file name of all matching files. Wildcards are supported, so the command:

    $find /usr/tim -name foo* -print

finds all files with the first three letters "foo".

You can search the entire file system structure by specifying the root directory as the path. Thus, to find all occurrences of the file called "core", the command would be:

    $find / -name core -print

(Whenever a fatal error occurs in an application, UNIX writes a copy of the user's memory area to a file called **core**, which can be used by programmers and system administrators to trace the problem.)

With the above **find** command, UNIX starts at the root directory "/" and searches it and all its subdirectories recursively for files called "core". This usually covers the entire UNIX file system, and the **find** command has to perform a lot of work. With such a wide search scope, the command can take several minutes to operate, depending on the size of your UNIX installation. The **find** command also uses quite a lot of CPU power, so the system administrator may not appreciate you conducting too many **find** commands over the entire file system!

You can use the **find** command to identify owners of a file, using the **-user** option. The user ID of the owner is used as an argument. For example, the command:

    find /usr/tim -user tim -name foo* -print

looks for files starting with "foo" owned by "tim". A similar option is **-group**, which can be used with the name of a valid group.

Recently accessed files can be identified with the **-atime** option. This takes an argument for the number of days, and all files that have been accessed in that number of days, or fewer, will match. The **-mtime** option is the same, but applies to the modification date. The command:

    find /usr/tim -mtime 4 -name foo* -print

matches files starting with "foo" that have been modified in the last four days.

A full list of all **find** command options is shown in Table 7.4, although most of them are seldom used by a typical system user.

Linking Files Together (The **ln** Command)

The **ln** (link) command allows you to assign more than one name to a file. You use this when you want the same file to be referred to by several names. UNIX links the files together, so that using any of the linked names refers to the same file.

A couple of examples will help illustrate the use of links. Suppose you want to be able to execute the command **lc** by using the command **dir** (like DOS's directory command). UNIX does not have a command called "dir", so you could assign **lc** the name **dir** using the **ln** command:

    $ln lc dir

Then, whenever you type **dir** at the shell prompt, you will really be executing **lc**.

Another example is when you wish a file to be in two locations for ease of use. Suppose you have a file called "foobar" in "/usr/tim", but also want to be able to access it in the directory "/usr/tim/book". The command:

    $ln /usr/tim/foobar /usr/tim/book/foobar

shows the file in both directories, even though it physically resides in only one of them. It can be called up from either with equal ease.

Links do not create new copies of the file with new names, but rather, create new names that are maintained in the internal UNIX directory tables. You can assign as many links as you wish to a file. To determine how many links a file has, examine the listing output from the **l** (or **ls -l**) command. For example, the listing:

    -rw-r--r--   2 timgroup 34 Aug 01 11:50 foo
    -rw-r--r--   1 timgroup 34 Aug 01 09:59 foo2
    -rw-r--r--   2 timgroup 34 Aug 01 11:55 goo

shows the number of links immediately after the file permissions. The files "foo" and "goo" both have two links. In this case, they are linked together, but you can't tell this from the listing.

It is possible to find out what files are linked to which using the **-i** option with these commands:

    $l -i
    4510 -rw-r--r--   2 timgroup 34 Aug 01 11:50 foo
    4531 -rw-r--r--   1 timgroup 34 Aug 01 09:59 foo2
    4510 -rw-r--r--   2 timgroup 34 Aug 01 11:55 goo

The first column in this listing shows the i-node number (the i- node is an internal number maintained in the UNIX 'i-node' table where file information is kept). As both "foo" and "goo" have the same i-node, they refer to the same file.

UNIX uses links for naming directories. When you create a new directory with the **mkdir** command, UNIX assigns the name ".." to the parent directory, and the name "." to the current directory. This is true throughout the whole directory structure. You cannot change these names using **ln**.

More Ways to List Files (The **ls** Command)

In earlier chapters, you used the **lc** and **l** commands to obtain listings of the files in a directory. There are several variations of the list commands that are occasionally useful.

Most UNIX versions support a command called **ls** that works in much the same way as **l** and **lc** do. Some UNIX versions that support **ls** do not have both **l** and **lc** available. Whenever you see a reference to **l**, **lc**, or **ls** in this book, you can use any of the other list commands to accomplish the same results, although you may need some optional switches to get identical outputs. You have already seen this with the **l** command, which is identical to **ls -l**.

The **ls** command is widely available, and so will serve as a model for discussion. **ls** supports several options, which can be combined. The most important options are shown in Table 7.1.

Table 7.1: ls Options

Option	Description
-a	lists all files, including hidden files
-d	lists only directories
-l	produces a long list (like the l command)
-r	lists files in reverse alphabetical order
-t	lists files by date of last modification, from the most recent backwards. (Combined with the -r option, it lists from oldest to most recent.)

Table 7.1: *ls Options* (Continued)

Option	Description
-F	marks all directories with a backslash, and executables files with an asterisk
-R	lists files and directories recursively

You can combine any of these options in one command. You can also specify a file name after the options, which may include wildcards. For example, the command:

```
$ls -r /usr
```

lists all files in the "/usr" directory in reverse alphabetical order. If you do not specify a file name, UNIX assumes the current directory.

The asterisk wildcard tells UNIX that all files are to be matched. Interestingly, the commands **ls** and **ls *** are not the same, although their output may appear identical in many cases. The asterisk is a "metacharacter" that tells UNIX to consider each file as a match, and results in all directories beneath the current directory being expanded. You can see the difference by changing to the "/usr" directory and trying both commands.

Printing the Listing Commands

Directory listings can be redirected to a printer by several techniques, but two are commonly used. If you know the printer's device name, you can direct the information to it directly using the command:

```
$ls > /dev/lpt1
```

The actual printer device name would replace "/dev/lpt1" in this example. You can use any options after the **ls** command, as long as they precede the redirection symbol.

Directing the output of a command to a printer in this manner can cause problems, though. If the printer is being used by others at the same time, you can cause their output to be ruined, and sometimes the printer locks up.

It is much better to use the UNIX system's print spooler to send the output for you.

You can use the spooler **lp** for this by directing the output from the **ls** command to a temporary file. UNIX systems maintain a special directory called "/tmp" that is used for temporary files. The files in "/tmp" can be deleted after use, or they are removed automatically by the system at intervals.

You can use the "/tmp" directory as a place to store your output, which can then used by the **lp** spooler. The commands:

```
$ls > /tmp/a
$lp /tmp/a
```

create a file called "a" in the "/tmp" directory, then print it using the **lp** spooler. Again, you can use options and file names, if you wish, as long as they precede the redirection symbol.

Comparing Files (The **cmp** and **diff** Commands)

If you work on several copies of a file, it is possible that you will have two or more copies that may be different from each other. You can sometimes forget what the differences between the files are, but UNIX provides several simple commands that list the differences for you.

Suppose you are writing a document, and you have two similar files called "letter.1" and "letter.2". You used the "letter.2" file to try something different without destroying the main document contained in "letter.1". You can find the differences between these two files by using the **cmp** (compare) command:

```
$cmp letter.1 letter.2
```

If the two files are identical, **cmp** does not produce any output. If there are differences, the character and line number at which the first difference occurs is reported. At typical output from the **cmp** command might appear as:

```
letter.1 letter.2 differ: char 16, line 2
```

Only the first difference between the files is reported by **cmp**, which then displays the shell prompt character again.

The **cmp** command provides only two options, neither of which is used much except by programmers. The **-l** option prints the character number (actually, the byte number is reported) and the differing bytes (in octal) for each difference. For example, a sample output might be:

```
$cmp -l letter.1 letter.2
16   116  164
17   157  145
18   167  163
19    40  164
20   151   12
...
```

The **cmp** command also supports the **-s** option. It does not report any differences in files to the screen, but does provide a "return code" that can be detected and checked by a program. If the return code is 0, the files are identical. If it is 1, the files are different. A return code of 2 means one or both files are inaccessible or an argument was missing in the command line. When executed at the terminal, the **-s** option does not display anything.

Another, better program for determining the differences between files is the **diff** program. **diff** stands for "differential file comparator", and it indicates which lines must be changed in the files to make them identical. The **diff** program uses a reporting format that employs **ed** (editor) commands. An example of the use and output of **diff** is:

```
$diff letter.1 letter.2
1a2
> test
```

This shows that the word "test" appears on the second line of "letter.2" but not in "letter.1" (and hence should be added to make the first file identical). After each line of **ed** command, the actual line affected is shown. If the line is in the first file, it is preceded by the "<" symbol. IF it is in the second file, it is preceded by the ">" symbol, as in the above example. Each line that is affected in either file is reported in this manner.

A more complicated output is generated when there are several differences between the two files. If the "letter.1" file contains the following:

```
Now is the time for all good men to come to the
aid of their country
Blah Blah
```

and the "letter.2" file contains:

```
Test Test
Now is the time for all good men to come to the
aid of their country
```

then the result of the **diff** command for these two files will be:

```
$diff letter.1 letter.2
0a1
> Test Test
3c4
< Blah Blah
---
```

This shows that the "Test Test" line in the second document must be added to the first, and that the line "Blah Blah" must be deleted from the first.

The **diff** command supports several options to help determine the real differences in files. The **-b** option ignores trailing blanks, including spaces and tabs. This allows extra spaces after lines to be ignored for comparison purposes.

The **-e** option produces a script (program) file of commands that can be used directly by **ed** to produce identical files. The output should be redirected to a file to allow it to be used. The command:

```
$diff -e letter.1 letter.2 > changes
```

creates a file called "changes" that contains all the **ed** instructions for making "letter.1" look like "letter.2". The reverse can be accomplished (making "letter.2" look like "letter.1") by changing additions to deletions, and vice versa. Alternatively, the order of file names can be switched in the **diff** command.

Counting Lines, Words, or Characters (The **wc** Command)

A UNIX utility called **wc** is useful for counting the number of lines, words or characters in a file. The name **wc** stands for "word count", but the command can be used with arguments for the other items.

The **wc** command assumes that words are separated in text by a blank space, punctuation, tab, or new line character. To total the number of words in the file "foobar", the command and its output would be:

```
$wc foobar
85    349   2097 foobar
```

The numbers represent the number of lines, words and characters in the file, respectively. If you want just one of the three totals, use one of the "-l", "-w", or "-c" options. For example, to count only the number of words in "foobar", use:

```
$wc -w foobar
349   foobar
```

The response shows there are 349 words in the file. You can get two of the totals by specifying two options. If none are specified, **wc** assumes all three, as in the first example.

Sorting a File (The **sort** Command)

Sometimes you may want to arrange a file containing tabular data in order. UNIX's **sort** command allows you to organize any ASCII file into a sequence. (ASCII stands for the American Standard Code for the Interchange of Information; it assigns a decimal code to each letter of the alphabet and special character, so that they conform to a standard. Most computers use ASCII, because it allows their information to be read by others without translating.)

Suppose you have a file called "names" that contains the following list of names:

```
tim
bill
john
mike
debbie
joe
```

You can sort the name alphabetically and display the sorted results on the screen with the **sort** command:

```
$sort names
bill
debbie
joe
john
mike
tim
```

The original file is not changed, so to save the sorted list, you must redirect it to another file. Using the command:

```
sort names > sorted.list
```

saves the sorted names from the "names" file in another file called "sorted.list".

The **sort** command has a number of options to specify the type of sorting sequence required. When no other format is specified, **sort** uses ASCII, which corresponds to alphabetical order, with uppercase coming before lowercase. Valid **sort** options are shown in Table 7.2.

Table 7.2: sort Options

Option	Description
-b	ignores any leading blanks
-c	checks that the file is already sorted
-d	sorts in dictionary order
-f	ignores case
-i	ignores non-printing characters
-n	orders numerically

Table 7.2: *sort* Options   (Continued)

Option	Description
-r	reverses the comparison order
-o	sends output to a specified file
-u	unique occurrences: ignore duplications of entries

The **-b** option ignores any spaces or tabs that may precede the line to be sorted. If there are spaces before the first character, the **sort** program treats the space as important, and sorts it as such. The **-b** option tells it to ignore these leading blanks and use the next "real" letter, number, or special character.

The dictionary-order sort selected with the **-d** option uses digits and letters, but ignores case. In other words, "Tim" and "tim" are treated as the same, which would not be the case if ASCII sequence were followed (uppercase letters come before lowercase in ASCII). Only letters, numbers, and blanks are important in dictionary order.

The **-n** option places all non-numeric entries first in the list, then those entries that have numbers next, ranging from smallest to largest.

The **-u** option prints only one entry when there are more than one of the same kind. This results in a shorter output file if there are duplications.

Although the output of the **sort** command can be saved in a file with the usual UNIX redirection command, the **-o** option specifically forces the output to a file, the name of which is given in the **sort** command line.

Several switches can be used to combine options. The **sort** command can also be used with other commands, using redirection or piping. For example, the command:

```
$who | sort
```

displays an alphabetical list of the users currently logged on the system, piping the output of **who** to **sort**, which displays the sorted list on the screen.

Searching for Patterns (The **grep** Commands)

UNIX provides three commands for searching through files for specific strings. These commands have unusual names: **grep**, **egrep**, and **fgrep**.

The **grep** command finds and displays all matching occurrences of a string within a file or set of files. Suppose you have written a document called "letter":

```
Dear Sir:

I hope you are well.
Please send any books you have on UNIX.
After all, UNIX is a wonderful operating system.
It is much better than any other I have tried.
I am rapidly becoming a UNIX expert.

Cheers,
Tim
```

You can print out all the lines in the file where the word "UNIX" occurs by using the command:

```
$ grep "UNIX" letter
Please send any books you have on UNIX.
After all, UNIX is a wonderful operating system.
I am rapidly becoming a UNIX expert.
```

You will notice that the string to be located comes first, followed by the name of the file or files. As shown above, only those lines that contain the specified string are listed.

The string to be found in this example has been enclosed by quotation marks to prevent it being confused with "metacharacters" by UNIX. UNIX interprets metacharacters differently than other characters. Metacharacters are any characters that have a special meaning to UNIX, such as the wildcard symbols "*" and "?". Other metacharacters include redirection, (>) piping, (|) and other reserved symbols for the shell programming language, and some application reserved characters.

In this case, the quotation marks around "UNIX" could have been ignored because the text contains no metacharacters. It is good practice, though, to always enclose literal text in quotation marks to avoid confusing and erroneous results from the **grep** command. It doesn't matter whether you use single or double quotes to indicate the literal text, as long as they are paired properly.

The **grep** command has two variants called **egrep** and **fgrep**. Each of the programs is a slight variation on the other, optimized for particular searching types. The **grep** command uses a small algorithm to find matches. **egrep** uses a fast algorithm, but can take up considerably more memory. **fgrep** is used primarily for finding strings, and is optimized for that purpose. All three use the same command formats and options. The options supported by **grep**, **fgrep**, and **egrep** are shown in Table 7.3.

Table 7.3: **grep** Command Options

Option	Description
-c	shows a count of all matching lines
-i	ignores case during comparisons
-l	shows only the names of files with matches in them
-n	precedes each line with its line number in file
-s	suppresses error messages
-v	displays all lines that don't match
-x	displays only exact matches of the entire line (**fgrep** only)
-y	ignores case

Using the same "letter" file as above will show the use of some of these options. The command:

```
$grep -c "UNIX" letter
3
```

shows that 3 lines in the file matched the specified string ("UNIX"). The line numbers for each of the matches can be shown with the **-n** option:

```
$grep -n "UNIX" letter
4:Please send any books you have on UNIX.
5:After all, UNIX is a wonderful operating system.
7:I am rapidly becoming a UNIX expert.
```

Instead of using the **grep** command, we could just as well have used **fgrep** or **egrep** and achieved the same results. The choice of the form of **grep** doesn't really matter until very large matching sequences are required. For example, to search the entire file system for a particular string would be considerably quicker with **fgrep** than either of the other two forms due to its optimized algorithm. (The search through the entire file system will still take a lot of time!)

Ideally, there should only be one **grep** in UNIX to cover all the search types, but it just isn't possible to make a small enough program that provides all the capabilities. Therefore, all three versions are provided with UNIX.

Using the UNIX Calendar (The **cal** Command)

UNIX has a calendar program called **cal** that is supplied as a basic utility. Typing **cal** at the shell prompt displays the calendars for this month, and the following and previous months.

The **cal** command can also take arguments for a month and year, so the command:

```
$ cal 5 1958
May 1958
 S  M Tu  W Th  F  S
             1  2  3
 4  5  6  7  8  9 10
11 12 13 14 15 16 17
18 19 20 21 22 23 24
25 26 27 28 29 30 31
```

prints the calendar for May, 1958.

The **cal** program is quite versatile when it comes to specifying the month and day to be printed. Normally, **cal** expects the month to be a digit (from 1 to 12, of course). However, it can understand such arguments as "Jul 1917". The year must always be fully specified. Thus, if you enter the command:

```
$cal jul 17
```

you get July, 17 AD. To obtain a full year's calendar you do not specify a month, just the year.

Creating Date-Based Reminders

You can use the **cal** program to send yourself reminders about specific dates. If you create a file in your home directory called "calendar", with a list of dates and appointments, the system automatically scans the file for today's date, and sends you a mail reminder if any of your appointments match.

The layout of the "calendar" file must specify the month and day, and the text of the message. The year is assumed to be whenever the specified date occurs next, unless explicitly given. A sample "calendar" file might look like this:

```
1/12    Brian's Birthday
2/30    Joe's Birthday
5/7     Wedding Anniversary
3/21    Mom's Birthday
9/21    Next chapter of book due
10/12   Doctors appointment
```

Each line has the date and the message that is supposed to be sent to you when **cal** scans the file. When January 12th occurs next, for example, the calendar program routes mail to you that contains the message "Brian's Birthday".

Table 7.4 lists all the find options available to you.

*Table 7.4: **find** Options*

Option	Description
-a	time nfile was accessed in the last n days
-c	time nfile had its inode changed in the last n days
-exec cmd	executes 'cmd' if the search is successful
-group	name has group 'name'
-links x	file has x links
-mtime n	file was modified in the last n days
-name	file matches 'name'
-newer	file was modified more recently than 'file'
-perm	perms has permissions that match octal 'perms'

Table 7.4: *find* Options (Continued)

Option	Description
-print	prints pathname
-size n	file is n blocks long
-size nc	file is n characters long
-type x	file has type 'x' (b,c,d,p or f)
-user	name has owner 'name'

Table 7.5: Summary of Commands

Command	Description
cal	displays a calendar
calendar	checks date for triggered events
cmp	compares files
diff	displays the differences between files
egrep	string search
fgrep	string search
find	finds a file
grep	string search
ln	links several filenames to one file
l	directory list
lc	columnar directory list
ls	directory list
sort	arranges entries in a file in order
wc	counts words, lines and characters
who	shows users currently on the system

Chapter 8

The Shell

What Is a Shell?

When you log in to a UNIX system, you are automatically using a *shell* program. A shell is a program that acts as the interface between you and the operating system. It interprets the commands you enter, and translates these into the correct commands for the operating system to execute.

More than simply acting as a translator for your commands, a shell offers a simple interactive environment that acts as a window into the UNIX system for you. The shell also provides a powerful development language, which you can use to write complex programs without really knowing anything about programming languages.

The UNIX system is composed of a large number of small programs that can accomplish single tasks efficiently. Working in UNIX is simpler than in many other operating systems because all of these existing tools can be used together. Output and input from one command can be directed to other commands with a minimum of effort.

With the large number of programs already available in UNIX, you do not have to worry about many of the smaller parts of a large task. Indeed, a single command line in UNIX can itself call many megabytes of existing programs.

Most high level languages (like C, Pascal, and Structured Basic) require a procedural approach. In other words, a programmer has to write in detail the exact steps required for a program to execute. The UNIX shell, which is a non-procedural language, requires the programmer to indicate the desired result without getting into all the steps needed to accomplish the task.

As an example, suppose you were writing a program in C and needed to sort a long list of variable names. Unless you can call a custom library written by someone else, you have to decide on the sorting algorithm to use and write the program code yourself directly into the application (or pull it from some other program you wrote that does that). With UNIX, you simply call **sort** and ignore how it all gets done.

Programs written in the shell language are sometimes called *shell scripts*. A script is a list of commands for the shell to execute.

The UNIX Shells

UNIX uses three main shells, which have slightly different characteristics. The most widely available is called the Bourne Shell, and is distributed with virtually every UNIX system available. Two enhanced versions of the Bourne Shell have appeared, called the C Shell and the Korn Shell. These add extra capabilities to the Bourne Shell, albeit at an increase in shell program size and execution time.

The choice of shell may be made for you by your system administrator, or you may be allowed to determine which will best suit your needs. All of them use the same basic structure, and differ primarily in the way a programmer would use them. If you do not intend to write programs, the choice of the shell is not really important. For those intending to write programs, choosing the correct shell can greatly increase productivity. We will examine the different shells in more detail later.

A quick note on shells: all shells, and many other UNIX programs, have the ability to *fork*. A fork is when one program or process creates another one. The ability to fork is very important in an operating system.

The PATH

Each user is assigned a series of subdirectories that they have access to. You can tell UNIX to examine not only your current directory for the program when you type in a command, but others too. The other directories to be searched automatically for your commands are included in a list called the *PATH*.

The path each user has may be different. Most users search the "/bin" and "/usr/bin" directories, which are where the UNIX programs usually reside.

You can look at your path by typing the command **set**:

```
$set
HOME=/usr/tim
LOGNAME=tim
MAIL=/usr/spool/mail/tim
PATH=.:/bin:/usr/bin:.
PS1=$
PS2=>
TERM=ansi
```

One of the lines begins with the word "PATH". This is the *system variable* (a string reserved for use by the shell) that contains your path. Following the equal sign is a list of directory names, separated by colons. Each directory in this list is searched for the program to execute when you enter a command.

In the example above, the path contains the current directory (signified by the period), "/bin", and "/usr/bin". After receiving a command, the shell searches each, in order, until it finds the program. If it cannot find the correct program in the path, it tells you it could not find the program.

The other lines that appear when you type **set** show other system variables. "HOME" tells the shell where your starting (home) directory is.

"LOGNAME" is your login name. "MAIL" gives the directory and name of your mail box. "TERM" is the type of terminal you are using.

The "PS1" and "PS2" system variables are the prompts that are displayed by the shell. The first one, PS1, is the shell prompt character. If you change this to something else, your shell prompt will similarly change.

You can try this with the following commands:

```
$PS1="Hi There! "
Hi There!
```

The second line, which you may at first think is just an echo from your command sent, is the new system prompt!

Some systems may not respond with a change in the prompt, but display the old prompt character again. If this is the case, you must instruct the shell that it is to use the new character in place of the old one. Simply redefining the string is not enough on all systems, as some use a safeguard to prevent accidental reassignment of system variables. To force the shell to recognize the new value of PS1, enter the command:

```
$export PS1
```

Until you log out, or change the prompt again, the new prompt will be displayed every time the shell waits for you to type something. You could use **vi**, **ed** or some other editor to permanently change the value of "PS1" by editing the file called ".profile" in your home directory. We will discuss this file in more detail in the next chapter.

The "PS2" prompt is displayed whenever you start a new line in an uncompleted command. You use the "\" character (the opposite slash to the one you use for naming directories) to indicate to the shell you have more to type on a second line, and that the shell should not process what you have entered so far.

For example, suppose you wanted to get the **word count** of a file called "letter", but you put the command on two lines instead of one (remember you changed the PS1 prompt above!):

```
Hi There! wc \
> .letter
120   582     1521      letter
```

When you enter the backslash, the shell displays the PS2 character to indicate that it is waiting for a continuation of the previous line. You can change this prompt to another character (or characters) in the same manner as you changed PS1.

Wildcards

Many UNIX commands require arguments such as file names or options. In an earlier chapter, you saw the use of the wildcard symbols "?" and "*" to match single characters and all characters, respectively. UNIX has a wider variety of wildcards that add extra versatility to your commands.

You can specify a range of valid values using square brackets. For example, the pattern:

```
[a-m]
```

matches everything between lowercase "a" and lowercase "m", inclusive. The dash character tells UNIX that anything between the preceding and following characters is valid. The pattern:

```
[a-enz]
```

tells the shell to match everything between "a" and "e" inclusive, as well as the letters "n" and "z". If you only wanted to match vowels, you would use the pattern

```
[aeiou]
```

You can use these ranges with any UNIX command that can take an argument such as a file name. The command:

```
$l [a-m]etter.*
```

might result in the following output:

```
-rw-r--r--  1  tim   group     1872 Aug 01 02:45  better.news
-rw-r--r--  1  tim   group     7364 Jul 23 17:12  letter
-rw-r--r--  1  tim   group      723 Aug 15 01:46  letter.tom
```

Similarly, the following example shows the use of two ranges in a single command:

```
$l [a-djmtw]e[a-u]ter*
-rw-r--r--  1  tim   group     1872 Aug 01 02:45  better.news
-rw-r--r--  1  tim   group    19823 Aug 08 12:01  debters
```

Numbers can be used in ranges, too:

```
$l chapter.[1-5]
-rw-r--r--  1  tim   group 234563 Jun 12 12:12  chapter.1
-rw-r--r--  1  tim   group 127327 Jun 23 09:53  chapter.3
-rw-r--r--  1  tim   group  83762 Jun 28 18:01  chapter.4
```

Ranges are usually used when a file name is expected, but you can use them in other circumstances—to give search ranges, for example.

Pipes and Redirection

You have already seen UNIX's powerful redirection and piping capabilities. These functions come up in any discussion of the shell, so we will briefly review them here.

Input for a command can be read from a file by using the UNIX symbol <, as in this example:

```
$command < file
```

The "<" character tells UNIX to read the input for "command" from the file called "file". Similarly, you can send output from a command to a file using the > symbol:

```
$command > file
```

This places all output from "command" into a new file called "file", erasing any previous contents. You saw examples of this in earlier chapters when we used **cat** to save to a file. For example:

```
$cat > newfile
one
two
three
<Ctrl-D>
$wc newfile
    3       3      14 newfile
```

To append data to an existing file, you can use the >> symbol:

```
command >> file
```

This sends the output of "command" to be appended to the end of the file called "file". Continuing with the above example:

```
$cat >> newfile
six
seven
<Ctrl-D>
$wc newfile
    5       5      24 newfile
```

Output can be sent from one command to be the input of another using the "pipe" symbol | with the following format:

```
$command | command2
```

which sends the output of "command" to the input of "command2". An example is the command:

```
$who | wc -l
      5
```

this sends the output from the **who** command to the **wc** command. The -l option counts the number of lines from the **who** output, in this case 5, and displays it. This shows the number of users on the system.

All of these operations can be combined in one command line, as in the following example:

```
command1 < file1 | command2 | command3 > file2
```

This reads the input for "command1" from "file1", and moves the output of this command to the input of "command2". "command2", in turn, sends its output to the input of "command3". The output from "command3" is saved in "file2". While it is unlikely you would ever have to use a command of this complexity, UNIX will not stop you from trying.

Part of the power of UNIX is derived from the capability to perform all these redirections. As a command is processed from left to right, the transformation of data can be accomplished using existing UNIX tools, instead of having to write many small programs or using temporary files.

Metacharacters

In UNIX, characters like >, <, |, *, ?, [, and] are used as symbols for various operations. You will have seen all of these in earlier chapters. These symbols are called *metacharacters*. If you want to use one of these characters specifically in an argument and not have it interpreted as a metacharacter (having special meaning), you must precede it with a backslash. The backslash tells UNIX to take the character literally, not as a shell metacharacter.

The command:

```
$echo > start
```

opens a new file called "start" and then closes it, so it contains only a new line character. But if you want to echo the string "> start", then the > character needs the backslash:

```
$echo \> start
>start
```

This results in the string "> start" being echoed to the screen or default device. The shell will ignore the backslash when processing the command, but recognizes that it must treat the following character as a literal character, and not as a shell symbol.

If you want to use a backslash as a literal character, you must supply two of them. The shell ignores the first, and treats the second as a true backslash.

Using backslashes in long commands with more than one metacharacter can be awkward, so shells provide a way of indicating that a whole string is to be treated literally. Enclosing the string in single or double quotation marks accomplishes this. The command:

```
$echo 'these are no longer metacharacters \ / * $ < >'
```

results in the entire string being treated as though the symbols are characters, and not metacharacters.

Creating a Shell Program

The steps to creating a shell program are simple: First, write the shell commands in a file, then make the file executable. The shell program can be written with any word processor or editor, as long as strange formatting commands are not left in that would confuse the shell. The commands can even be typed into a file from the terminal, using **cat**, although this is difficult to do without mistakes when the file is lengthy.

To make a shell file executable, use the **chmod** command:

```
$chmod +x filename
```

"Filename" is the file containing the shell commands. You can then run the program by simply typing its name. (This is assuming you don't change directories. If you do, UNIX may not be able to find the program without its full pathname.)

The entire operation can be demonstrated by creating a small shell script that will count the number of users on the system. The **who** command will create a list of the users, and this will be moved as input to **wc**, using the -l option to determine the number of lines.

The example below uses **cat** to create the file, which is called "users". After the command line has been typed, the file is saved using a Ctrl-D sequence.

```
$cat > users
who | wc -l
<Ctrl-D>
$chmod +x users
$users
19
```

When executed, the shell program "users" tells us that there are nineteen people logged in to the system.

The Bourne, C, and Korn Shells

The Bourne Shell is supplied with virtually every UNIX system available. Originally written by Steven Bourne in the language Algol (C was not yet widely accepted), it was later rewritten in C and has been improved steadily over a period of several years.

The Bourne Shell is a program called **sh** (short for shell). When you log on to a UNIX system, it starts the **sh** program for you unless the system administrator has set up a different starting shell or application.

The C Shell, called **csh**, was designed to make the interface to UNIX look as much like the C language as possible. For this reason, it is favored by C programmers. The C Shell also adds a few new features to the Bourne Shell. Three of the most important are *history, aliasing,* and *job control.*

History is the ability of the shell to remember previous commands that you have typed, and allow you to recall them or modify them quickly without having to retype. This is very useful when you have complex or lengthy commands. The history capabilities of the C Shell take a little while to learn, but are very useful when you use the same commands (or slight variations of commands) repeatedly.

Aliasing allows you to redefine commands using another name. For example, instead of having to type **ls -l** every time, you could redefine the command with the name **dir**. You may think that this can be done with **ln** (linking), but **ln** only works on single names and does not include arguments. Aliasing allows long command lines with several parts to be referenced as one command.

The final important new feature of the C Shell is job control. This allows you to control several processes at once. In earlier chapters, we discussed the ability to send tasks for background processing. Once a process has been sent to the background, it stays there. With job control, you could pull any of your background tasks into the foreground and monitor or interact with them, then send them to the background again. This is like having several active processes running at once, and allows you to switch between them all easily.

The C Shell changes the shell prompt character to a percent sign, instead of the Bourne Shell's dollar sign. Many systems have both shells available, so you can try the C Shell by typing **csh** at the prompt:

```
$csh
```

To return to the Bourne Shell, you will have to enter a Ctrl-D sequence:

```
%<Ctrl-D>
$
```

The C Shell sounds more powerful than the Bourne Shell, and it is. However, the extra capabilities are not without a price. The C shell is harder to learn than the Bourne shell. It is also larger, so it executes a little slower.

The Korn Shell (**ksh**) was written later than the C Shell. It is not a standard part of most UNIX systems, so must be purchased and installed separately. The Korn Shell was designed to take advantage of the best features of the C Shell without adding all the complications that the C Shell introduces. The Korn Shell was designed to be compatible with the Bourne Shell, so programs written in the Bourne Shell will work with the Korn Shell. In contrast, Bourne Shell programs will not work with the C Shell in most cases.

The Korn Shell prompt is usually the same as the Bourne Shell's. For this reason, it is sometimes hard to remember which shell you are in when you have both available. A simple way is to type the **alias** command. If you get an error, you are in the Bourne Shell. If you get a list of system variables, you are in the Korn Shell.

The Korn Shell adds the C Shell's aliasing, job control and history features, but in a slightly different manner. The C Shell tries to look and act like a C program. The Korn shell doesn't, and so is easier to work with than the C Shell.

The Korn Shell adds new features that both the Bourne Shell and C Shell do not have. The Korn Shell is again larger than either, and so is a little slower. If it is available on your system, it is probably going to be a better shell for you to work with than the Bourne or C shells (unless you plan to do a lot of C programming).

Chapter 9

Getting to Know the Shell

This chapter introduces programming the shell. Although some programming experience is useful, it is not necessary in order to understand the concepts presented here. For those who have never programmed before, however, there is a lot of material. Do not be too alarmed if you get lost; with practice, the concepts will fall into place.

Shell programs are usually referred to as *shell scripts*, which is the term we will use here. We have already seen a script in the last chapter, where we created a new file called "users" to tell us how many people were using the system. That script used two UNIX programs (**who** and **wc**). Scripts are collections of UNIX programs, sometimes with other commands added, as we will soon see."

This chapter presents scripts and script fragments that you may not fully understand at first glance, but the primary aim is to illustrate different flow control commands. After completing the chapter, you should be able to understand all the code.

For the most part, the scripts presented in this chapter run in the Bourne Shell, as it is the most commonly used. They will also run in the Korn Shell, as it is compatible with the Bourne Shell. C Shell users will have to change some program instructions.

Shell Variables

In the last chapter, we discussed system variables. PATH and TERM are examples of system variables. Variables are also used to hold values within the shell. *Shell variables* are always stored as strings (characters), and are valid only while the shell that defined the variables is active. As soon as the shell program terminates, the variables and their values are lost. However, any program that was called by the shell can use the shell variables. Don't get too confused about the terms **variable** and **string**. A variable is something that holds a value (numbers or letters) that can change (hence are variable). Variables are always named something, so that they can be used by referencing their name. Strings are simply a bunch of characters (such as letters) that are thought of as one item (hence a string of letters).

The value of a variable is used whenever the variable is called with a dollar sign ($) in front of it. For example, if you define the variable "FOOD" as holding the value "hamburger" and then call $FOOD from a program, the string "hamburger" is substituted. If you leave off the dollar sign, the shell thinks you are talking about the name "FOOD" instead of its assigned value. The dollar sign tells the shell to "use the value of the variable".

You can see this by defining a variable called "USERS" to hold the string "who".

```
$USERS=who
$USERS
USERS: not found
$$USERS
root       tty01      Aug 02 14:10
tim        tty02      Aug 02 16:23
tom        tty1a      Aug 02 18:35
```

When you type USERS without the dollar sign, UNIX interprets the command as "USERS", and tries to find a program with that name. With the dollar sign in front, the shell replaces the variable with its value, and executes the **who** command.

Variable Types and Assignments

Positional Variables There are three types of shell variables. *Positional variables* are determined by the command line. *User-defined variables* are used for storing strings for the user. *Predefined special variables* are variables used only by the shell.

The shell creates *positional variables* when you enter commands on the command line. This is best shown with a simple example. The command:

    $l letter.1 letter.2 foobar test.c

has five parts to it. The first is the command itself (l). The second is "letter.1", third is "letter.2", and so on. Each part of the command is assigned a number by the shell that corresponds to its position.

The shell begins with the number 0. Each part of the command is given a variable name with its number, symbolized by the dollar sign and the number. The positional variables for the above command are:

    $0   l
    $1   letter.1
    $2   letter.2
    $3   foobar
    $4   test.c

By starting with the number 0, the shell actually has the variable $1 refer to the first *argument* in the command line.

Positional variables are numbered consecutively from the start of the command line, and refer to the argument number, or position, in the command of each piece of the command. The shell resets the counter to zero every time a new command is executed. Positional variables are used mostly in shell programs, but they can be used for other purposes.

Positional variables stop numbering at $9. They can be defined higher, but this requires a bit of a programming trick to accomplish. The command:

```
$more a b c d e f g h i j k l m n
```

results in the value "a" assigned to $1, "b" to $2, and so on up to $9. In this example, you have nine positional variables defined (one for each letter of the alphabet) so that $1 is "a", and $9 is "i". You cannot access $10, as the shell interprets that as the value of $1 with a zero after it.

UNIX provides a command called **shift** that allows you to move the positional variables down in sequence. The **shift** command drops the first value ($1), and moves all the others down one. Using the positional variables just mentioned, after one **shift**, $1 contains "b", and $8 is now "i". The ninth positional variable, $9, is now free to have the value "j".

You can deliberately assign a positional variable with the **set** command. If you enter the following command:

```
$set joe tim john
```

the shell assigns "joe" as $1, "tim" as $2, and "john" as $3. You cannot redefine $0 in this manner, as $0 is usually reserved for the name of the command. Values assigned by the **set** command are effective until another **set** command, or reassignment due to execution of a shell command.

User-defined Variables *User-defined variables* are assignments made by a user. You define these variables by entering the name you want the variable to assume, an equal sign, and the string the variable is to hold. For example:

```
UNIX="fast"
```

assigns the string "fast" to the variable called "UNIX". You should not put spaces around the equals sign in a variable assignment, or the shell assumes you are trying to execute a command.

Variable names can contain letters, numbers, and underscores. They cannot begin with a number, so must use a letter or an underscore for their first character.

You can define several variables at the same time. For example, the command:

```
UNIX="fast" DOS="slow"
```

results in the variable "UNIX" being assigned the string "fast" and "DOS" being assigned the value "slow". You must take care to put a space between the two definitions, or the shell will not interpret the command completely.

When defining several variables, you should bear in mind the shell's processing order. It works from the right of the assignment command line to the left, so the command:

```
UNIX=$DOS DOS="slow"
```

results in "UNIX" being assigned the value "slow". This is because of the right-to-left assignment rule: "DOS" is first defined as "slow", then "UNIX" is defined as the value of the variable "DOS".

You may have noticed that in the example above, all the assignments are in quotation marks. This ensures that the shell interprets the entire value literally, and avoids translation of metacharacters. If you make the assignment

```
UNIX="very fast and efficient"
```

the string "very fast and efficient" results whenever you call $UNIX. If you leave out the quotation marks, only the first word is assigned, so that "UNIX" has the value "very".

When quotation marks are used to assign a value, any valid characters can be enclosed in the assignment. Characters such as tabs, control codes, and UNIX metacharacter codes (like the pipe and redirect symbols) are all taken literally.

Wildcards, as used in pattern matching, are not supported in variable assignments, so the command:

```
star=***
```

results in the variable "star" being assigned the string "***". You will notice we used lowercase for the variable name. There is no need to stick to uppercase, and you are free to mix case as you wish. You could have placed quotation marks around the three asterisks, and the result would have been the same. However, as you have already seen, the two commands:

```
star=*** ***
```

and

```
star="*** ***"
```

are *not* identical, as the space in the first assignment causes only three asterisks to be assigned.

The use of double quotation marks (") is significant. Single quotation marks actually inhibit substitution of a variable's value. The command:

```
UNIX='$star'
```

results in the variable "UNIX" being assigned the value "$star", not the value of the variable "star". This is a very common mistake made by users beginning to learn shell programming.

You can use variables inside an assignment to another variable. If you enter the following commands:

```
UNIX="fast"
DOS="not so $UNIX"
```

the value of "DOS" is "not so fast". The shell replaced "$UNIX" with its value, as indicated by the preceding dollar sign.

If you want to assign a variable within a string, but also add some text in the same string, you can embed the variable name that is to be substituted in braces. For example, if you assign the variables:

```
e="UNIX is fast"
f="$eest"
```

the variable "eest" is not defined properly. The shell cannot find a value to substitute for the entire string "eest". The shell will substitute a null value when the variable is not defined. The command:

```
f="${e}est"
```

results in the desired assignment of the string "UNIX is fastest" to variable "f". You use the braces to differentiate the variable name to be substituted.

Predefined Variables   *Predefined variables* are special variables, such as HOME and PATH, that the shell understands. You have already seen these in earlier chapters. There are many shell special variables, but the most common are shown in Table 9.1.

Table 9.1: Predefined Variables

Variable	Description
HOME	defines your login directory
IFS	internal field separator character
MAIL	pathname for your mail box
PATH	directory search list for commands
PSI	primary prompt string
PS2	secondary prompt string

Recall that the prompt strings determine the prompt that is displayed when you are using the shell. You learned how to change them in the last chapter.

On some UNIX systems, shell variable definitions are not automatically assigned to the shell when you type them. A specific command must be used to tell the shell you wish the reassignment to be made. This command is **export**. All shell special variables must be **export**ed before they can be recognized by the shell.

When you redefine shell variables, each should be **export**ed. You can **export** them one at a time, or do several at once with a single command line. If you redefine the six shell variables above, the command:

```
$export HOME IFS MAIL PATH PS1 PS2
```

reassigns them all with one command. More than one variable can be assigned on a single line, as long as there is a separator (in this case a space) between them.

Some special variables are reserved for the shell only, and cannot be reassigned by the user. They can be used in a program to help monitor its condition. The special shell variables are used primarily by programmers. The dollar sign ($) holds the number of arguments passed to the shell on a command. You saw positional variables earlier in this chapter, which use the dollar sign and a number for each argument on the command line. If you enter the command:

```
$more a b c
```

the value of the dollar sign is set to three. The positional variables are assigned so that $1 is "a", $2 is "b", and $3 is "c". The dollar sign by itself is useful for checking that a user has supplied the correct number of parameters required by a program.

The shell variable "$?" contains the exit code (also called a return code). This is a number that is generated by any command when it finishes to indicate whether it was successful or not. If the command executed properly, the "$?" variable has the value zero. If the result is non-zero, an error occurred. The exact value of the return code can help indicate what type of error occurred.

The shell variable "$$" contains the process id (PID) of the current process. Each process on a UNIX system has a unique number, so this allows a programmer to check on the status of the process and stop it if necessary. A related shell variable called "$!" contains the process ID of the last process to run in the background. (You may recall the ampersand (&) tells UNIX to run a program in the background.)

Finally, a shell variable called "$-" contains a list of the execution flags used in the shell. This is not used very frequently, except when debugging programs.

The .profile File

When you log in to UNIX, the **login** program reads a special file in your home directory called **.profile**. The period at the start of the file name identifies this as a "hidden" file. It will not show up in a normal listing using **l** or **lc**. You can access this file, though, and list its contents using **cat** or **more**.

The **.profile** file contains one-time commands that are executed before you see the shell prompt character. These commands set up the shell variables such as PATH and MAIL, and export them. It can also define variables used by applications.

You can examine your **.profile** file when you are in your home directory to see the variables defined for you:

```
$cat .profile
:
#.profile
# (there may be a lot of copyright information here)
#
PATH=$PATH:$HOME/bin:.
MAIL=/usr/spool/mail/'logname'
export PATH MAIL
```

Your **.profile** will undoubtedly be different, and may contain other commands as well. The example above sets two system variables (PATH and MAIL), then **exports** them. The PATH assignment itself uses a reference to $PATH, which is a default path set by your system administrator. The MAIL command uses another substitution for "logname". This is your user name, and is assigned when you log in.

Additional lines may be in your **.profile** that define your file creation mask (sets the permissions your files acquire), terminal type, or other system-dependent information.

When a shell starts a program, it passes all variables that are assigned through the **export** command automatically. You can get a list of the variables that are set this way by simply typing **export** at the command line. It responds with a list that looks similar to this:

```
export MAIL
export TERM
export PATH
export TERMCAP
```

You can also see all the variables that have been defined by typing **set**, which may result in a long list being displayed on your console.

Shell Program Flow

When a shell is scanning a command line, it follows a specific order of operations. First, the shell reads the line up to the first semicolon or newline character, and treats that much of the command as a separate command to be dealt with.

The shell then analyzes the command. This action is called *parsing*. All variables are replaced by their assigned values. If any single or open quotation marks are in the command line, the shell attempts command substitution. Next, the shell scans for redirection instructions. If there are any, the shell performs and then ignores them.

At this point, the shell has a command line with all substitutions conducted and all redirection commands active. It then reads the whole line looking for internal field separator (IFS) characters, which would tell the shell to break the line into distinct arguments. IFSs are used to break commands into smaller parts to be recognized as words, switches, or other indicators. The default IFS is a space. If any metacharacters are used, these are expanded. Finally, the resulting command line is executed.

Most programs involve more than a simple list of valid UNIX commands. Program flow may involve *loops, branching,* and *testing of variables*, with different actions depending on the outcome of the test. These changes in the top-to-bottom flow of the program are "flow control" commands.

Flow control commands allow a program to perform more than a simple list of commands one after another. Flow control allows a program to change to different parts of the program depending on some tests or values that are set within the program.

Any line beginning with a pound sign (#) in a shell script is a *comment line*, and is ignored when the program is executed. It is useful to use comment lines where applicable in code to explain what is going on to others who may read your program. They also help you when you have to return to the program to change it.

The **test** Command

Many of the programs that follow use the UNIX **test** command. It is worthwhile examining it now, to avoid confusion later. The **test** command checks a condition to see if it is valid. If it is valid, **test** sends a return code of zero. If it is false, a return value of one is sent. These return codes are referred to as 'true' and 'false', respectively.

The **test** command evaluates a condition given as an argument based on an option that must be specified. The most frequently used **test** options are shown in Table 9.2:

Table 9.2: **test** *Options*

Option	Description
-r file	true if 'file' exists and is readable
-w file	true if 'file' exists and is writeable
-x file	true if 'file' exists and is executable
-f file	true if 'file' exists and is a regular file
-d file	true if 'file' exists and is a directory
-u file	true if 'file' exists and its user-ID bit is set
-g file	true if 'file' exists and its group-ID bit is set
-s file	true if 'file' exists and its size is not 0
-z s1	true if the length of string 's1' is zero
-n s1	true if the length of string 's1' is not zero
s1 = s2	true if strings 's1' and 's2' are identical

Table 9.2: **test** Options (Continued)

Option	Description
s1 != s2	true if strings 's1' and 's2' are not identical
s1	true if 's1' is not the null string

There are also algebraic **test** statements, as shown in Table 9.3:

Table 9.3: Algebraic **test** Statements

Statement	Description
n1 -eq n2	true if integers 'n1' and 'n2' are equal
n1 -ne n2	true if integers 'n1' and 'n2' are not equal
n1 -gt n2	true if integer 'n1' is greater than 'n2'
n1 -ge n2	true if integer 'n1' is greater than or equal to 'n2'
n1 -lt n2	true if integer 'n1' is less than 'n2'
n1 -le n2	true if integer 'n1' is less than or equal to 'n2'

Finally, any of these tests can be negated (reversed) by an exclamation mark before the test. Some examples of the use of **test** will be shown in the following discussion of flow control statements.

The **if** Statement

An **if** command instructs the shell to test the statement after the word **if** and see if it is valid. In computer terms, if the test is valid, it is "true". If it is not valid, it is "false". If the test is true, the commands that should be executed are shown after the word **then**. This is best remembered as "if this is true, then do what follows".

The shell provides an **if/then/else** construct that can be used in any shell script. The format of the **if** statement for the Bourne Shell is:

```
if <test>
then <command>
else <command>
fi
```

fi indicates the end of the **if** construct. The **else** is optional.

You can write a quick example of this construct by using the UNIX **test** command. When the **-r** option of **test** is used, the program checks to see if the file name following it exists. The program:

```
# test whether the file "letter.1" exists
if test -r letter.1
then
    more letter.1
fi
```

uses **test** to see if a file called "letter.1" exists. If it does, it is displayed on the screen by the **more** command. If "letter.1" does not exist, nothing happens.

You might have noticed that the line with the **more** command on it is indented slightly. These indentations make the entire program easier to read by graphically showing you where the logic statements (such as **if**) are, and the commands that occur between them. With large programs, indenting the code properly can make an amazing difference in the readability of the program.

You can enter this program using an editor or word processor, and save it under a suitable name. Then, you can use the command by making it executable. If you forget to do this, you will get a message from the shell:

```
execute permission denied
```

Remember, the command to make the file executable is:

```
chmod +x filename
```

The simple program you wrote above can be elaborated slightly to make it more informative by using the "else" statement.

```
# test if a file exists
if test -r letter.1
then
    more letter.1
else
    echo "The file does not exist!"
fi
```

This program displays the message "The file does not exist!" if the file "letter.1" cannot be found.

If you added the two new lines to the first program above, and kept the same program name, you may have noticed that you do not have to use **chmod** again to make the program executable. Because you are editing a file that is already executable, it remains executable, regardless of how many times you change it.

Instead of testing for just the one file, you can make the program much more useful by supplying the name of the file to be tested for as a positional variable. The changes to the program are not complex:

```
# test whether the file "letter.1" exists
if test -r $1
then
    more $1
else
    echo "The file $1 does not exist!"
fi
```

In this program, the $1 positional variable holds the name of the first argument in the command line when you execute your program. Suppose you called the program "testit" (you can't call it **test** as that is already a UNIX program name!), and want to test for the file "letter.2". The command is:

```
testit letter.2
```

and $1 takes the value "letter.2". You can try entering the program name without an argument. The shell responds with the message:

```
testit: test: argument expected
```

If you give the command more than one argument, only the first is recognized by this simple program.

If/else commands can be *nested* many levels deep. That means that you can have an **if** statement inside another one. You may want to do this to test another condition on the same file, or for some completely different test. Suppose you want to have the file displayed only if it is not of length zero (contains nothing). Then the program could be written as:

```
# test if a file exists
# and has a length greater than zero
if test -r $1
then
    if test -s $1
        then
            more $1
    fi
else
    echo "The file $1 does not exist!"
fi
```

As you can see, the second **if** loop is nested inside the first. If the first **if** statement is true, the program then goes to the second **if** statement and tests that one.

In the example above, if the second statement is not true, nothing happens because there is no **else** statement. The first loop's **else** won't be executed either, because the first part was true. Indenting the statements help you to visualize where each control flow statement begins and ends.

Suppose you want to put a second **if** loop after the **else** statement. There are two ways you can do this. The first way uses a separate **if** statement just as in the previous example.

```
# test if a file is a directory
# if not, test whether it is a file, and display it
if test -d $1
then
    echo "$1 is a directory!"
else
    if test -f $1
        then
            more $1
    else
        echo "The file $1 does not exist!"
    fi
fi
```

This program checks first to see if the argument is a directory. If it is not, then the program tests whether it exists at all. If the file exists, the program uses **more** to display it. If the file doesn't exist the program prints a message.

The shell can save you a little time when using this kind of **if** statement layout. Instead of nesting one **if** below the **else**, the shell has a special command called **elif** that combines the two:

```
# test if a file is a directory
# if not, test whether it is a file, and display it
if test -d $1
then
    echo "$1 is a directory!"
elif test -f $1
    then
        more $1
    else
        echo "The file $1 does not exist!"
    fi
fi
```

The **elif** command saves a line of typing, but more importantly lets the shell program run a little faster. It also can be easier to read when there are a lot of commands in a program.

You can nest **if** loops several deep, but it can become very difficult to track the logic of a program when you use too many. In cases where several **if** statements are required, the shell's **case** statement should be used instead.

The *case* Statement

The **case** statement allows you to perform several tests without writing a lot of confusing control structures (like nested **ifs**). The format of the **case** statement is:

```
case    value    in
    choice1)   commands ;;
    choice2)   commands ;;
    ...
    choicen)   commands ;;
esac
```

"Value" is a variable that is tested for matching each of the "choice"s. The keyword "in" at the end of the case statement is necessary.

Each "choice" is checked in order, with the "commands" that follow executed if "value" matches "choice". The two semicolons indicate the end of the commands for each match.

You can use the **case** statement when a user must choose from a list of choices, as in the following short menu example:

```
# example of case statement usage
# this uses a simple menu, followed by the case choices
echo "Enter the number of the program you wish to run:"
echo "1 - who"
echo "2 - date"
echo "3 - pwd"
echo "4 - cal"
read choice

case $choice in
      1)    who ;;
      2)    date ;;
      3)    pwd ;;
      4)    cal ;;
      *)    echo "That wasn't a valid choice!" ;;
esac
```

This program shows several things you have not seen before. First, you can see how the menu is displayed on the screen with the **echo** commands. Then, the program waits for the user to type something in, which is stored in the variable "choice". The **read** statement waits until something has been typed, followed by a Carriage Return.

The **case** loop lists each choice and the action to be taken if it matches "choice". The dollar sign in front of "choice" makes sure the shell uses the value of "choice", not the string 'choice'.

The asterisk that is the last of the options in the **case** statement will match whenever one of the other choices does not match. In this case, if a user doesn't enter a number between one and four, the asterisk command is used.

while and *for* Loops

Sometimes, you may want to have the shell repeat a loop several times until some condition is met. This is called *conditional looping*, and the shell allows you to do this in two ways.

The **while** loop continues to execute as long as some test is true. The **while** loop has the format:

```
while condition
do
        commands
done
```

which executes "commands" as long as "condition" is correct.

The following simple example of the **while** command accepts input from the user at the terminal and then echoes it straight back until the user exits the program by typing Ctrl-D or pressing Del.

```
# sample while program loop
# gets variable INPUT from the keyboard
while read INPUT
do
        echo $INPUT
done
```

The input is assigned to the variable "INPUT" by the **read** statement. Output uses the **echo** statement to recall the contents of the variable INPUT (remember—the dollar sign calls the value of the variable, instead of assuming the literal string "INPUT" is to be echoed).

The shell has a similar conditional loop called **for**. The **for** statement's syntax is similar to the **while** statement:

```
for variable in list
do
        commands
done
```

This executes "commands" as long as "variable" is found in "list". When a positional variable is used in the program, the shell allows you to drop the "in list" part of the structure. This can be more clearly explained with a couple of examples.

First, a program similar to the **while** statement program above can be written using the **for** statement. Here, a positional variable is used, so the "in list" part of the command is dropped.

```
# sample 'for' program
# reads from the command line and echoes back
for word
do
   echo $word
done
```

You could have used the variable "INPUT" again, but this example shows that you can use lowercase for variable names, if you want.

The program reads positional variables from the command line, and **echoes** them back to the screen until there are no more. The **for** loop continues only as long as there is a variable assigned to "word".

This program is used by typing its name with arguments. If the program is called "listem", you see:

```
$listem bill bob john
bill
bob
john
```

It echoes arguments back until they are all used up.

You can use the **for** loop with the "in list" portion of the statement in another example. The following program reads an input from the keyboard and generates a reply.

```
# example of 'for' loops using lists
echo "Hi!  What is your name? "
read INPUT
for i in $INPUT
do
echo $i
done
echo "That's all folks!"
```

This program, called "names", asks the user's name, then displays the parts of the name (if more than one part is input) on separate lines until all the parts are used up. A final message is generated. Here is how "names" works:

```
$names
Hi!  What is your name?
James Michael George Ebenezer Smith
James
Michael
George
Ebenezer
Smith
That's all folks!
```

In the program, a **for** statement reads the list of names held in INPUT. The letter "i" is simply another variable that marks the position of the shell as it reads along the names.

Breaking a Loop

A **while** or **for** loop continues to execute until the conditions in its statement are not met. There may be cases where you will want to terminate the program prior to the conditions being true. You can do this with the **break** command.

Also you can force another *iteration* (repeat) of the loop using the **continue** command. Both the **break** and **continue** statements must be within the body of the loop they apply to. The **break** command stops iteration of the loop it is embedded within, while **continue** reiterates the loop it is embedded in.

The following skeletons show the actions of the two statements:

```
while true
do
    commands
    if <test>
    then
        break            -----------      the break command
    fi                            |       breaks the do loop
    more commands                 |       and moves to after
done                              |       the done statement
more commands        <-----------
```

```
while true            <-------------      the continue
do                                  |     skips to the
    commands                        |     next cycle of
    if <test>                       |     the while loop
    then                            |
        continue      --------------
    fi
more commands
done
more commands
```

Both the **break** and **continue** commands are useful when used carefully. The **break** command is handy for getting out of test loops such as **case**.

Finally, the **exit** command terminates execution of a program wherever it is placed. It stops the shell executing the program, and the shell prompt character is re-displayed. You can use the **exit** command anywhere inside a program, as many times as you wish.

Getting Proficient with Shell Programming

It is beyond the scope of this book to go into more detail about shell programming. In this chapter, you have seen examples of the basic statements that are used in programming, but there is much more to learn. However, with the material above and a little practice, you will be able to write large programs that allow you to accomplish amazing things using the shell.

Chapter 10

Basic System Administration

Every system requires at least one person who understands both the hardware and the software to ensure that the machinery is operational on a day-to-day basis. This person, who is usually also responsible for allowing users to access the system and for performing backups of the storage media, is called the *system administrator* or *system manager.*

Most small UNIX systems require that only one person has the capability to perform system administrator duties, although it is good practice to have two people capable of performing the tasks. That way, if one person is unavailable, another will be able to maintain the system.

In most cases, the job of the system administrator is not time-consuming. Seldom will it take more than a few minutes per day (especially with small UNIX systems) so it is not necessary to assign someone exclusively to the position. UNIX systems can be maintained quite readily by anyone who wishes to perform the tasks.

The system administrator's tasks are numerous, but they are all fairly simple. A system administrator is typically responsible for:

- ensuring that the system is working correctly
- keeping the system available through the work period
- performing system backups
- installing new applications or updates
- managing the file systems ("housekeeping")
- maintaining user accounts
- adding new devices (printers, terminals, etc.)
- optimizing performance whenever possible
- keeping a system log
- performing system diagnostics regularly
- providing UNIX support to users

In addition, the system administrator traditionally acts as the first line of help for a user with a problem, and should have access to technical manuals, application support telephone lines, and other resources. New users, especially, look to the system administrator to help with problems.

This chapter examines the hardware and peripherals a system administrator must control. The creation of users, terminal characteristics, and backup systems are all discussed here. Additionally, the system administrator is responsible for managing the individual processes UNIX runs, both for itself and for users. In this chapter, we will concentrate first on the physical system, or hardware.

The Superuser Account

Every computer system, regardless of its size or complexity, must have some means for a system administrator to access every aspect of the hardware and software. With UNIX, this is accomplished with a special login that provides the administrator with unlimited access to the operating system, and no concerns about file access. This account is called the *superuser*, and is normally activated by the user name 'root'. A password is assigned to the account in much the same way as with any user account.

The superuser can move through every file system on the computer with the capability to override all file permissions settings. Due to this power and the chance that a superuser will inadvertently issue some command that will damage the system (such as deleting a system file), the superuser account should be used only for system maintenance functions.

It is not advisable to use the superuser account as any user's general account.

The system administrator will of course know the superuser password, but should have a user account for daily use. Many system administrators operate from the superuser account all the time because of its power, but many know from bitter experience how this can lead to problems! Only those who need to perform system administrator tasks should know the superuser password, and this information should be kept carefully restricted.

Starting and Stopping the UNIX System

One of the most important things a system administrator has to know is how to start the UNIX system. Starting the system is also called *booting* it. It is also necessary to be able to stop the system correctly, in order to prevent damage to files. Stopping the system is called *shutting down*.

Starting the System

Upon starting, the UNIX operating system performs several tasks. First, it reads the loading instructions from the boot device (sometimes a floppy, but most often the primary hard disk). These instructions are normally written as the first sector on the boot device, and the instructions are called the *bootstrap* (from the old cliché about pulling yourself up by your bootstraps). The bootstrap instructions provide the commands to read the essential parts of the UNIX operating system into RAM.

When the UNIX system is turned on, it displays a prompt similar to:

```
Boot
:
```

Then it waits for the user to tell it where to look for the boot information. When in regular use, the boot program has a default setting that reads the information from the primary boot device, and this can be triggered by simply pressing Return.

As UNIX is being loaded, diagnostic messages may be relayed to the screen. After the operating system is loaded, UNIX may perform a check of the file system to determine if the system was improperly shut down prior to this boot. If it was, the file system must undergo a process called "cleaning" to reset the table information and ensure that files are not damaged. If it is necessary for UNIX to clean the system, it displays the prompt:

```
Proceed with cleaning (y or n)?
```

Answering 'y' and pressing Return initiates a program called **fsck** (file system check) that attempts to repair damaged files, delete those that cannot be repaired, and clean up all internal tables. If the system is not cleaned, it is possible that file errors will develop due to inaccurate file-table data.

Choosing the Operating Mode

Following the completion of **fsck**, or the loading of UNIX if the system did not need cleaning, the system asks the user to indicate the type of operation required. UNIX has two operating modes—*normal* and *system maintenance.* Under normal operation, the system runs fully, allowing users to log in and execute applications. System maintenance mode allows the system administrator to work on the operating system directly, without allowing access to others at the same time.

To determine the mode UNIX should be in, a message similar to the following is displayed:

```
Type CONTROL-d to continue with normal startup,
(or give the root password for system maintenance):
```

If you press Ctrl-D, the system continues to load the operating system and initialize devices. UNIX then executes a series of instructions in a start-up file, usually called "/etc/rc". When the system is fully initialized, the **login** prompt appears on all currently attached terminals.

To access the system under system maintenance mode, you must enter the superuser or root password. The system then displays the superuser prompt "#" instead of the usual shell prompt character ($ or %). In this case, the "/etc/rc" file is not executed. To move from the system maintenance mode to normal operations mode, pressing Ctrl-D to start the remainder of the loading as if it had been entered at the mode prompt.

Each UNIX system has one terminal or screen that is usually directly connected to the main unit. When system maintenance mode is entered, only this single terminal is active. The rest do not display UNIX prompts until the full UNIX system is loaded. This terminal is called the *main console* or *primary terminal*.

Shutting Down the System

Computer systems must be stopped and turned off occasionally. This can be for moving, to add hardware, in case of impending electrical problems, or for any number of other reasons. It is not a good idea to simply turn the power off on a UNIX system that is running, as this can cause many problems with interrupted processes and corrupted file systems.

The UNIX operating system can be stopped by two methods. The **shutdown** command terminates all running processes as neatly as possible, without cutting everything off arbitrarily. When you execute the **shutdown** command, it sends a message to all logged-in users that the system is going to terminate, and then begins to close off the processes. Once activated, **shutdown** should not be interrupted. After **shutdown** has completed closing all the processes, it locks the hard disk heads in their parked position.

The **shutdown** command allows an argument that tells it the number of minutes to wait before shutting everything off. For example, the command:

```
shutdown 4
```

tells the system to shut down in four minutes. Some versions of UNIX do not allow arguments for the number of minutes, while some insist on a value. If the number of minutes is not supplied as an argument, UNIX will ask for the number of minutes to shutdown. In most versions, **shutdown** can only be typed at the main console by someone logged in as **root**.

Some versions of UNIX also have a command for immediately stopping the system. When the **haltsys** command is issued, all users are immediately logged out, and the system shuts down. Any work in progress is immediately lost, but the file systems can be rapidly shut down without damage.

It is best to precede the **haltsys** command with a couple of **sync** commands, as in:

```
# sync
# sync
# haltsys
```

The **sync** command updates the file system tables immediately, and flushes any buffers. If **sync** is not used, file system integrity cannot be assured. The second **sync** is just extra security: It is not really needed, but "makes sure". The **shutdown** command calls **sync** automatically.

Moving to System Maintenance Mode Without Rebooting

It is occasionally necessary to disable the normal operation of the system, and "drop down" to the system maintenance mode. This may be done for tape backups, for example, if you want to make sure no one modifies files during the backup process.

You can always get to system maintenance mode by shutting the system down and then starting it up again. If you give the superuser password at the mode prompt, you will enter system maintenance mode. This process is somewhat time-consuming.

To drop to system maintenance mode directly, a superuser can use another argument with **shutdown** in most versions of UNIX. The command:

```
shutdown su
```

causes **shutdown** to act as if the whole system were being terminated normally, but instead of completely closing the system down, it drops the system to maintenance mode, displaying the "#" prompt. After a **shutdown su**, normal operations can be re started with Ctrl-d.

Maintaining File Systems

UNIX revolves around file systems, so one of the system administrator's tasks is to keep them well organized. Because UNIX requires a considerable amount of *disk I/O* (input/output), user files, and *disk swapping* of processes, a fast, well-organized hard disk is important. Swapping is when the hard disk is used as an extension of system memory. UNIX will write the contents of memory to a temporary file, and read in another file containing different memory contents. The memory is swapped with a disk file.

Ideally, hard disks should never exceed 85 percent of capacity. In other words, 15 percent of the hard disk should always be kept free. UNIX needs this free space for temporary files. If more than 85 percent of the disk space is used, UNIX becomes extremely sluggish. Eventually, the system can reach a condition called *thrashing*, in which the operating system spends so much time trying to swap parts in and out of the disk that nothing else occurs.

Once a hard disk is completely full, with no free space available, UNIX ceases trying to write to the disk. Any user files or processes that involve disk access simply stop.

How to Keep Space Free

The system administrator can monitor the amount of disk usage with a number of commands. If the disk begins to fill up, and reaches or exceeds the recommended 85 percent capacity, direct action should be taken to free some space.

The easiest ways to maintain free space are to regularly remind users to remove unwanted files, or to let the system administrator archive files that should be kept but are not needed on a regular basis. Many system administrators simply send electronic mail at intervals or when a file system is filling up, and find that the users get into the habit of keeping their user areas clean of old material. Sometimes it may be necessary to approach individuals whose areas are occupying large amounts of space and show old file dates, and be a little more insistent.

Many UNIX systems keep several versions of an application in backup subdirectories, which can be deleted. Seldom used or redundant applications and programs can be archived for storage and then deleted.

UNIX and its many applications use temporary files a great deal. These are mostly stored in two subdirectories called "/tmp" and "/usr/tmp". The **/etc/rc** program, which is run when the system starts, usually contains instructions to delete the information in these areas, but when the system has been running constantly for many days, files can accumulate. The **cron** program can be used to activate a cleanup of the temporary areas at selected times, allowing UNIX to delete files there daily, or at some other interval. We will look at **cron** shortly.

Another source of useless files is the *core dump*. Whenever a critical error has occurred, UNIX saves a copy of the memory in a file called "core" in the current working directory of the user. On systems that have programmers developing applications or running poorly behaved applications, core dumps can occur frequently enough to be a small percentage of the available disk space.

A **cron** program can be used to locate all occurrences of "core" by using a **find** command that outputs to a file. Then, the file can be used as input to delete all these occurrences. A simple script file takes care of this. The command to use the **find** program to find all occurrences of the "core" file is:

    #find / -name core -print

Some applications use the temporary file areas to save working copies of files, which may be used in case of system crashes. The system administrator should be aware that automatic deletion of these directories may prevent a user from retrieving a copy of a damaged file. Each application should be checked so the system administrator is aware of how it uses the temporary subdirectories.

On the author's system, **cron** runs such a cleanup process, first deleting the "/tmp" and "/usr/tmp" directories, then locating and deleting all "core" files once a day, in the small hours of the morning. The system checks to ensure that no users are logged in and using the files before it executes the deletions (otherwise, the users' processes may crash).

Log files are often used by the system administrator to keep track of users, and monitor system usage. These files should occasionally be checked by the system administrator and deleted if they begin to outgrow the system. A log file may be emptied but not deleted by moving its contents to "dev/null" using the command:

```
#cat < /dev/null > file
```

where "file" is the name of the log file.

If space problems are chronic and continuous, the system administrator will have to seriously consider adding another hard disk, or changing the programs maintained on the system.

Checking the Free Space

The system administrator can rapidly determine the amount of free space on the system by using the **df** (disk free) command. **df** reports the number of blocks or sectors that are unused. If the system administrator knows the size of a block (usually 512 bytes), then the actual amount of disk space available is readily determined by arithmetic.

The example below shows **df** issued from the root directory of a 150 MB disk:

```
# df
/              (/dev/root ):      33034 blocks    23536 i-nodes
```

This tells you that there are 33,034 blocks free. Assuming you have 512-byte sectors, there are approximately 15 Mb of free space (or ten percent, which is less than the ideal number, prompting immediate file cleanup).

A variation on the **df** command displays the amount of used space, free space, and the percentage used:

```
# df -v
Filesystem        Mounted on        blocks      used      free    %used
/                 /dev/root         250670    216770     33900      86%
```

To obtain information about the amount of space used by each directory, issue the **du** (disk usage) command. If you specify a directory, the program returns the information for that directory only:

```
# du /tmp
50          /tmp/wp
52          /tmp
```

The format of the **du** response is simple. The first column reports the number of files and directories in that directory, and the second column gives the directory name.

If you specify the "/usr" directory, then all subsidiary directories below "/usr" are also reported. The **du** command by itself reports everything from the root directory, down, so entering it is the same as entering "du /".

Maintaining User Accounts

User accounts allow a system administrator to control access to the system. Ideally, each user who is allowed to use the system has a unique user name and password. The system administrator is responsible for creating the user names, and maintaining the user list to keep it current. Additionally, user groups can be assigned to allow users with similar access requirements to be logically grouped together.

User Groups

User groups allow several users to share files and directories, while those outside the group may not be allowed access. When first installed, UNIX provides a default group called "group" and leaves it up to the system administrator to create and maintain any other groups.

A user may belong to one or more groups. Groups are typically set up to reflect a company's organizational structure. In other words, groups may be created for the shipping department, administrative staff, order processing, and so on. Each group may have access to the files and programs needed for that department's use only. Supervisory personnel may have access to more than one group or all of them.

UNIX keeps track of groups in a file called "etc/group". There is no automated procedure with most UNIX versions for maintaining groups. The system administrator usually must use a text editor to modify this file.

To maintain groups, the system administrator must be logged in as the superuser. The information in "etc/group" has the following format:

```
groupname::groupID:usernames
```

A sample extract from this file would appear similar to:

```
research::50:tim,bill,dave,mark
shipping::70:tim,mike,bob
accounts::100:tim,debbie,sarah
```

To add a new group, the system administrator needs to decide on the group name, and a group ID number. Group names may be up to eight characters long. Group ID numbers are between 50 and 30,000. Both the group name and group ID number must be unique.

The new group is added by editing the "/etc/group" file and typing in the new information. All users who belong to the group should be listed, with their user names separated by commas. The new group becomes functional as soon as the file is saved.

After one or more new groups has been added, a program called **grpcheck** can be run that scans the "etc/group" file for correct format. If an error was made during the addition of the new information, **grpcheck** provides messages to that effect.

Users belonging to more than one group must use the **newgrp** command to switch groups. UNIX does not keep track of all groups a user belongs to, and uses the current group as the default for assessing file permissions.

Adding a User

Users are added to the UNIX system with the **mkuser** (make user) command, which must be executed by the superuser. When a user is created, UNIX performs several tasks, including adding information about the user to the userlist file (usually "/etc/passwd"), creating the home directory, creating a mailbox, and setting up a login initialization file (".profile" or ".login" depending on the shell).

mkuser issues a series of requests at the terminal. First, it asks if you want detailed instructions about the program:

```
#mkuser
Add a user to the system
Do you require detailed instructions? (y/n/q)
```

Entering "y" displays a screen of information about the **mkuser** command.

A series of questions is then displayed. The first asks whether you want to use the next available user ID. If you respond "n", you are asked for the ID number you wish to use. If you respond "y" to use the next available user ID, the system assigns the next number in its list. By choosing IDs specifically, a logical grouping can be set up for billing or tracking purposes, but most system administrators simply use the next available ID.

The **mkuser** program then asks for the new user's login name:

```
Enter new user's loginname, or enter q to quit:
```

It is best if user names have some consistency. Many system administrators simply use the user's first name or a combination of the first and last names. The first initial and full last name (e.g., tparker) seems to be the most popular naming method. It is convenient for both the users and the system administrator if the name is descriptive enough to allow identification of the logged-in users simply from their user names.

Names can be (almost) any length, but remember that users have to type their names frequently, so excessively long ones should be avoided.

After the user name is supplied, the **mkuser** program asks for the group the person is to be assigned to:

```
Do you wish to use the default group? (y/n/q)
```

The default group has the name "group", and the group ID number "50". If the default group is not accepted, the system responds with a list of the existing groups and asks the system administrator to choose the correct group for the user (or type in a new one). After the name of the group, a group ID number is requested.

Once you have established the group, the system prompts for the user's initial password:

```
Enter at least 5 characters for the password.
Enter password:
```

The initial password will probably be changed almost immediately by the user, so the choice of the first password is not worth belaboring. In many cases, the system administrator either repeats the user's name, or gives a single password to all new accounts (e.g., "password") and then tells the user to change the password on first access.

A password does not have to be supplied. If none is specified, the **login** program will not request a password when the user logs in. Some UNIX versions will display a password prompt even if no password is assigned. The user hits Return to indicate a null password in these cases.

After the password, **mkuser** requests the default shell type. A list of the shells currently on the system is displayed, and the system administrator must enter the number for the one to be used as the user's default shell.

Finally, the **mkuser** program allows you to enter a comment. The comment is often used for the user's full name or a department identification. Up to 20 characters are allowed for the comment, so only a bare minimum of information is possible.

After all this has been entered, **mkuser** displays the selected settings and asks if the information is correct. If it is, the data is saved and the new user becomes effective immediately. If the data needs editing, the system allows modification of any of the information.

The **mkuser** program creates the user's home directory, writes a ".profile" or ".login" file, and sets up a mailbox for the new user.

Removing a User

The system administrator can remove a user's account from the system with the program **rmuser**. Before **rmuser** can completely delete the user from the system, the user's home directory must be empty.

To remove a user, log in as the superuser and issue the command:

```
#rm -r homedir
```

to remove all files from the home directory, "homedir", and its subdirectories. You may recall that the "-r" options performs a recursive removal, deleting all files and subdirectories in the current directory. Next, empty the mailbox for the user with the command:

```
cat /dev/null > /usr/spool/mail/username
```

This removes all text from the user's mailbox.

Following this, execute the command **rmuser**. The program prompts for the user name that is to be deleted and asks for confirmation. Then the **rmuser** program sends a message indicating either that the command has been completed successfully, or indicating why it could not be performed properly. The most common reason for unsuccessful removal of a user is that the home directory has not been cleared.

Changing a User

Occasionally, a system administrator must change a user login ID and details about that user. There is no built-in method for performing a change, in most UNIX versions except to edit the user file. For the sake of illustration, assume this file is called "etc/passwd" and that the system you are working on uses a file layout similar to SCO XENIX's. Because this file is so important, you should make a copy before editing:

```
#cd /etc
#cp passwd passwd.old
```

Then invoke an editor and edit the file. The format of the "/etc/passwd" file is as follows:

```
username:password:IDnumber:groupID:comment:homedir:shell
```

where "username" is the login name, "password" is the encrypted password, "IDnumber" is the user's ID number, "groupID" is the group ID number, "comment" is any comment attached to the user, "homedir" is the user's home directory, and "shell" is the shell that is executed for that user. A sample entry is:

```
tim:j8.IJMJeFrHfU:201:50:Tim Parker:/usr/tim:/bin/sh
```

If you only need to change the user name, then replace the old user name with the new one. Similarly, changes in the home directory, comments, and shell can simply be typed in. All system accounts are assigned user numbers less than 200, and these should not be edited.

Do not attempt to alter the password. It is encrypted, and you can damage the user's account if you change it. If it is changed by accident, remove the password by changing it to nothing, leaving just two colons:

```
tim::201:50:Tim Parker:/usr/tim:/bin/sh
```

Be sure to remind the user to change the password with **passwd** at the next opportunity. The superuser can also change a password with the command:

```
#passwd username
```

and enter a new password for the user. Although it is practically impossible to decipher the encryption and replace the changed password with the correct version again, you can check the backup copy of the file for the correctly encrypted password.

If any problems occur when the user next tries to log in, it probably means the format of the edited line is wrong. You must either correct it, or use the old copy of the file to start the process again. UNIX provides a **pwcheck** command that checks the format of the edited file.

If the user name has been changed, the ownership of the files and directories must be changed to reflect this. You use the **chown** command to assign the files and directories to the new user name. (The **find** command can be used to locate all files that belonged to the old user ID.)

To change the user's group ID you need to know the group ID number of the new group and enter this in place of the old group ID number.

Using .profile or .login

Whenever a user logs in to the UNIX system, an *initialization file* is read and executed. For the Bourne Shell, this file is called ".profile", while the C Shell calls it ".login". In either case, it is an ordinary text file composed of valid UNIX commands to be executed when the user logs in.

Although the contents of the file will change depending on the version of UNIX and the defaults set by the system administrator, a typical ".profile" file appears as follows:

```
:
#
#     ...several lines of copyright information
#
```

```
PATH=/bin:/usr/bin:$HOME/bin:         # set command search path
MAIL=/usr/spool/mail/'logname'        # mailbox location
umask=022                             # set file creation mask
eval 'tset -m ansi:ansi -m :\?ansi -r -s -Q'
export PATH MAIL
```

PATH and MAIL tell UNIX where to look for files and where the mailbox location is. These are sent as defaults to the operating system for that user with the **export** command on the last line.

The **umask** command sets the file permissions default, which we will examine later. The **eval** statement with its rather complicated argument is used to determine the type of terminal the user is on. If the system administrator wishes to eliminate the terminal-type question during login, the terminal type should be entered in the file "/etc/ttytype" (we look at this in chapter 12) and the ".profile" or ".login" file edited to replace the long **eval** statement with:

```
eval 'tset -s'
```

or simply

```
tset -r
```

which uses the default terminal type from the "/etc/ttytype" file as the terminal type. In this case, the user will not be asked for their terminal type.

The system administrator can add to the ".profile" or ".login" file any additional commands to be executed when the user logs in. Suppose, for example, that the commands **who** and **lc** are to be executed whenever the user logs in. The system administrator edits the ".profile" or ".login" file and appends these two commands after the last line. When the user logs in, these commands are executed, and then the shell prompt character appears.

If there is a list of several commands the system administrator wants executed during login, it is easiest to create a new file containing these commands and assign it a single name. This name can then be placed in the ".profile" or ".login" file.

It is also possible to force a user to execute only one program and then log off. This is accomplished with the **exec** command. Suppose, for example, that the application the user is to access has full menu systems, and there is no need for the user to ever see a UNIX prompt. The application can be executed automatically from the ".profile" or ".login" command, and after exiting, the user will be logged out. Appending the command:

```
exec progname
```

to the ".profile" or ".login" file accomplishes this task. It is important to know that it is difficult (if not impossible) for the user to get to the UNIX prompt when the **exec** command is used in this way, so the application had better provide all the capability the user will need!

Copying Files with **copy** and **cp**

The **cp** command copies files, using the format

```
cp source dest
```

which copies "source" to "dest". The destination can be either a new file name, or a directory. When a directory is specified, the file name is assumed to be the same as the source's.

The **copy** command copies one or more files, directories or file systems. It can create directories to satisfy the command, when needed. The format of **copy** is similar to **cp**:

```
copy option source dest
```

with the addition of several options, or switches, from Table 10.1.

Table 10.1: ***copy*** *Options*

Option	Description
-a	asks the user for confirmation before copying
-l	uses links instead of copying when possible
-n	requires a new destination: do not overwrite
-o	retains original owner and group information

Table 10.1: *copy* Options (Continued)

Option	Description
-m	changes modification date and time to copy time
-r	recursive directory copy
-ad	asks for confirmation of directory copy
-v	verbose: displays file names as copied

When destination directories and files do not exist, they are created with the same permissions as the source. If both the destination and source are files, then **copy** acts the same as **cp**, which cannot copy entire directories recursively.

Automating Processes with **cron** and **at**

The **cron** program is designed to allow commands to execute at specific times without a user initiating them. **cron** is a clock daemon (a program that runs consistently in the background and performs a specific task), which reads dates and times in a file. When one of the file's entry's date and time matches the system date and time, **cron** executes the command.

Most system administrators use **cron** for regular maintenance functions such as tape backups, database reorganization, and file cleanups. **cron** is usually started when the system is booted, by an entry in the "/etc/rc" file. Unlike the **at** command, which executes commands only once, **cron** can execute the same command repeatedly. **cron** is available to all users.

UNIX provides a support program called **crontab** that enables a user or system administrator to manage **cron**, and to determine what is submitted and removed from **cron** execution.

Each user's **cron** information is kept in a separate file in the directory "/usr/spool/cron/crontabs". Each user who uses **cron** will have a file with their user name as the file name. System administrators usually use a file named "root".

The "crontab" files have a simple structure. Each file consists of one line for each process to be submitted. Each line has six columns separated by spaces or tabs. The columns, from left to right, represent the minute (0-59), hour (0-23), day of the month (1-31), month (1-12) and day of the week (Sun=0, Sat=7) that the program is to be executed on. The last column contains the command or script file that is to be executed.

Each column in the "crontab" file can contain a number in the range of valid numbers, two numbers separated by a minus sign to show an inclusive range, a list of numbers separated by commas to mean all of the values, or an asterisk meaning all legal values.

An example of a "crontab" file might look like this:

```
20  1  *  *  *    /usr/bin/calendar -
 0  2  *  *  *    /bin/organize_data
30  3  *  *  *    /bin/tapebackup
```

This executes the "calendar" program with "-" as an argument at 1:20 AM every day. We saw the **calendar** program in chapter 7. The command "calandar_" forces **calendar** to scan all user's home directories and send mail when matches are found. This saves each user from having to run **calendar** when they log on. Similarly, at 2:00 AM, a program or script file called "organize_data" executes, followed at 3:30 by "tapebackup". The commands used with **cron** can be either single commands such as "calendar", or script files that contain many lines of information, such as the last two lines in this example.

Users can determine what they have submitted to **cron** with the command:

```
crontab -l
```

This lists the **crontab** entries for the user. To remove a user's "crontab" file from the **cron** directory, use the command:

```
crontab -r
```

To submit a command to **cron**, the command is usually placed in a properly formatted file, then sent to **cron** with the command:

```
crontab file
```

When a new file has been saved, **cron** uses it automatically.

A system administrator can control who can send processes to **cron** with one of two files. The file "/usr/lib/cron/cron.allow" can contain a list of all users who can use **cron**. Alternatively, the file "/usr/lib/cron/cron.deny" can contain a list of users who are not allowed to use **cron**. Both files have one user name per line. If neither the "cron.allow" nor "cron.deny" file exists, only the superuser (root) can submit processes to **cron**. To allow global use of **cron**, an empty "cron.deny" file should be created.

On many systems, the system administrator can log all **cron** usage by setting the "/etc/default/cron" file to contain the word "YES" for the variable "CRONLOG". Then, all cron actions are recorded in a file called "/usr/lib/cron/log".

The **at** program is very similar to **cron**, except that it executes a command only once. You may recall that we looked at the **at** program in chapter 4. The format of the command is:

```
at time date file
```

The time can be specified as 1, 2 or 4 digits. One- and two-digit numbers are assumed to be hours, while a four-digit number is assumed to be hours and minutes. A colon may be used to separate the hours and minutes to make it unambiguous, if desired. A 24-hour clock is assumed unless "am" or "pm" is appended. (**at** also recognizes a few special words for times, such as "noon", "midnight", "now", "next", and "zulu" for GMT conversion.)

The date is an optional field. When a date is not supplied, the next time the specified time occurs, the command is executed. If a date is specified, it can be either as a month's name followed by a day number, or a day of the week spelled out or abbreviated to three characters. **at** recognizes two other words: "today" and "tomorrow". If desired, a year can be specified, but this is seldom required.

Just as with the **cron** program, you can obtain a listing of all processes submitted by **at** using the command

    at -l

and a process can be removed with the command:

    at -r

A user can only remove their own processes, except for the superuser, who can remove any.

The system administrator can allow access to **at**, or prevent access, using the same procedure as **cron**. The two control files are "/usr/lib/cron/at.allow" and "/usr/lib/cron/at.deny".

Processor Status

Every task that runs on a UNIX system has a process ID number assigned to it. It is useful to be able to determine which tasks are running for a number of purposes, including determining the load on the system, identify processes that are locked up, and seeing what background processes are running.

The **ps** (processor status) command allows each user to monitor their processes, or to list all system processes that are executing. The format of **ps** is:

    ps option

where "option" is any number of valid switches. The primary valid switches are shown in Table 10.2:

Table 10.2 Processor Status Options

Option	Description
-e	shows all processes
-d	shows all processes except process group leaders
-a	same as "d" but also ignores terminal processes
-f	generates a full listing
-l	generates a long listing

Table 10.2 Processor Status Options (Continued)

Option	Description
-t	shows a list of processes associated with a terminal
-u	shows a list of processes associated with a user
-g	shows a list of processes associated with a group

Terminal processes are those started by "getty", and one executes for each terminal enabled on the system.

ps provides a list of all processes that match the specified switches. The layout of the list depends on whether the "-f" or "-l" switches are active. A series of columns are displayed across the screen, each with a header. The headers and their meanings are given in Table 10.3, with the left column indicating which switches cause the column to appear:

Table 10.3: Headers and Their Meanings

Switch	Header	Meaning
l	F	status word (see below)
l	S	state of the process (see below)
f,l	UID	User ID of the process owner
all	PID	process ID number
all	PPID	process number of the parent process
f,l	C	processor utilization for scheduling
f	STIME	starting time of the process
l	PRI	priority of the process
l	NI	"nice" value for priority
l	ADDR	memory address or disk address of process
l	SZ	size in blocks of core
l	WCHAN	event for which process is sleeping (if any)
all	TTY	controlling terminal ID
all	TIME	cumulative execution time
all	CMD	command name (full command with '-f')

System administrators use **ps** frequently when a process has to be terminated. A frequent form of **ps** is:

    ps -ef | more

This uses both the full listing and all process switches. It is usually advisable, as shown here, to pipe the output to **more**, as there is seldom only one screen of information on multiuser systems.

The status word is a special flag that is associated with a process. There are five process flags used in the status word:

- 01   in core
- 02   system process
- 04   locked in core (for I/O, for example)
- 10   being swapped
- 20   being traced by another process

The state of the process is given by a single character. Valid process states are:

- B   waiting
- I   intermediate
- O   nonexistent
- R   running
- S   sleeping
- T   stopped
- W   waiting
- Z   terminated

The priority of a process is used to determine the execution order. The highest priority has the lowest number. If a process has been concluded but has a parent, and the parent has not accessed the child process, the process is marked as "<defunct>". A child process is one started by another process, which is called the parent process. this is also called **forking**. When one process starts another, it is said to have **forked**.

Terminating Processes with kill

You can terminate a process with the **kill** command. The format is:

```
kill -number processID
```

The process ID number can be obtained with the **ps** command. "Number" is an optional number specifying the signal number to be sent to the process. Signal numbers range from zero to fifteen, and default to 15, which is a terminate signal. Using the lesser value of 9 causes UNIX to try to gracefully exit an application, but may result in the process not being terminated.

Users can **kill** only their own processes, while a superuser can **kill** any process.

Chapter 11

Providing for Security

Security for a computer system has several meanings, ranging from determining who is allowed access to other users' files to protecting the system as a whole from malicious damage. The major concern of any security system is the prevention of damage to stored data. Many systems are just as concerned with who has access to data, as this may seriously affect both business and personal affairs.

Physical Security

The machines that are used to run the UNIX system can be protected from casual access by simply placing them behind a locked door. With the increasing miniaturization of hardware, special computer rooms are usually not maintained, but keeping the machines in a room or office that can be locked prevents the curious from "playing" with them.

All storage media, such as backup tapes, diskettes, or removable disk media, should similarly be kept locked up in nonmagnetic storage. Master disks for software are especially vulnerable with small systems, as the temptation for users to "borrow" disks to try on other systems increases with accessibility of the media.

The main computer console should never be left logged in, and it is a good habit to turn the console off when not using it. This will prevent the curious from trying to access the system from the main console.

Access Security

The main source of damage to computer systems is from unauthorized use of user accounts. Many users do not protect their passwords as well as they should, and tend to freely disseminate this information to others. Sometimes, unauthorized or unwanted system access is not directly linked to indiscretion with passwords: Many users simply walk away from their terminals for considerable periods of time without logging out.

The system administrator has to remind users continually that if they are leaving their terminals, they should log out. Not only will this prevent others from using their accounts, but it will also prevent unwanted "snooping" through personal files.

The choice of user passwords is also a subject worth discussing with users. Many use their spouse's name, their pet's name, or their date of birth as a password because it is easy to remember. It is also fairly easy for a knowledgeable and determined person to figure out. Random words or letter sequences are much more difficult, and use of these should be encouraged. Some system administrators do not allow users to set their own passwords, but supply them instead.

The superuser password is obviously the most critical password on the entire system. Although it is wise to let two people know this password, providing it to too many users may be fool hardy. Additionally, when you are logged in as the superuser, you must take care to ensure that you log back out to leave the terminal for even the shortest amount of time.

Write access to directories such as /bin, /dev, and /etc should be restricted to superusers. Users can have read and execute access, but there should be no need for a typical system user to write to any of these directories.

Despite constant reminders, users will occasionally leave their terminals while they are logged in. The system administrator can use several methods for monitoring this. The easiest is to use the UNIX **idleout** command.

Not all versions of UNIX offer the **idleout** command. If it is available, it is issued with an argument that specifies the amount of time a process can be idle (generating no activity) before it is terminated. For example:

    idleout 15

monitors the processes on the system, and when one has had no activity for fifteen minutes, UNIX terminates the process. Typically, if a user has not used the keyboard of a terminal for this amount of time, all of the user's processes are terminated, and the user is logged out. One problem with using **idleout** is that it indiscriminately kills all of a user's processes. If the user was distracted while in the middle of an application, and **idleout kills** the process, the user's work will not be saved automatically. This can cause a considerable amount of frustration among users.

Changing User Passwords

Users can change their passwords with the **passwd** command, but the superuser has an override capability to make changes without knowing the old password. In order to use this override capability, the superuser must include the user name:

    passwd username

You *must* be logged in as the superuser to do this. UNIX will request the new password twice, but will not ask for the old password as it does when you are changing your own password.

It is often a good security practice to force users to change their passwords regularly. This can be done with the **pwadmin** command. Each password on the system is dated, and when **pwadmin** checks these dates, it can force the user to make a change. This is referred to as *password aging*.

With **pwadmin**, the superuser can establish a maximum amount of time after which a user must change a password. The superuser can also specify a minimum amount of time before a user is allowed to change a password, but this is less often used. A superuser would do this to prevent users from changing their password once when forced to, and then immediately changing it back to the old password.

The **pwadmin** command can take several forms. Password aging can be invoked for a single user by using the command:

```
pwadmin -a username
```

The "-a" option tells **pwadmin** to use the default values found in the "/etc/default/passwd" file. These default values can be overridden by specifying "-min" or "-max" in the command line:

```
pwadmin -min time -max time username
```

where "time" is the number of weeks. Either "-min" and "-max" can be used together, or only one can be specified. The time in weeks must be between zero and sixty-three. (Obviously the maximum cannot be less than the minimum, nor the minimum greater than the maximum.)

Many system administrators find acceptable values for the minimum and maximum times to be two and eight weeks, respectively. This way, passwords are changed at least every two months.

Password aging can be disabled for a user with the "-n" option:

```
pwadmin -n username
```

A system administrator can force a password change for a user with the "-f" option:

```
pwadmin -f username
```

The user will be prompted for the password change the next time he or she logs in.

File Permissions In Detail

UNIX controls access to files and directories with *file permissions.* There are three different levels of permissions: *user, group,* and *other*. The *user* is the file or directory owner. *Group* refers to all users who are in the same group as the owner. *Other* refers to all users of the system; this level is also frequently referred to as *public.*

Permissions are displayed when the l command (or any similar command structure, such as **ls -l**) is issued. Ten characters show the permissions. The first character indicates the type of file. Valid file types are shown below in Table 11.1.

Table 11.1: Valid File Types

Character	File Type
-	Ordinary file
d	Directory
b	BlockI/O device
c	CharacterI/O device

Block and character I/O device files provide the operating system with instructions for accessing attached peripherals. Block devices communicate in discrete "chunks" of information, involving several characters of data and additional information indicating the start and end of the block. A typical block device is a hard disk drive. Character devices communicate one character at a time. A typical character device is a terminal.

The remaining nine characters indicate the permissions for user, group and other, in sets of three, respectively. The permissions are a combination of the valid characters shown in Table 11.2.

Table 11.2: Permissions for User, Group, and Other

Character	Description
-	No permission
r	Read permission: the file can be displayed or copied, or a directory can be accessed and its contents displayed

Table 11.2: Permissions for User, Group, and Other (Continued)

Character	Description
w	Write permission: the file can be modified. A directory write permission allows creation of files and directories within that directory
x	Execute permission (for files) or search permission (for directories): files can be executed, and directories can be entered with the **cd** command

A file can have the letters "rwx" in sequence for each of the three levels, or a '-' in place of any permission. By default, UNIX usually applies the following permissions to a file:

```
-rw-r--r--
```

This allows everyone to read the file, but only the user can modify it. (This is the default only if the user's **umask** is not changed; we will discuss **umask** shortly.) The default directory permissions are:

```
drwxr-xr-x
```

This allows everyone on the system to search and read the directory, but only the user can modify, create or remove files within it.

The File Creation Mask and umask

UNIX assigns each user on the system a default permission mask. This mask is represented by a three-digit number, with the digits representing user, group, and other permissions, respectively. The digits represent the permission that level will be assigned for all files modified by the user, and they are defined in Table 11.3.

Table 11.3: Permission Mask Digits

Digit	Definition
0	read and write (and execute for directories)
1	read and write
2	read (and execute for directories)
3	read
4	write (and execute for directories)

Table 11.3: Permission Mask Digits (Continued)

Digit	Definition
5	write
6	execute for directories
7	no permission

The default mask on most systems is "022", which provides the default permissions mentioned earlier.

You can change the file creation mask with the **umask** command, specifying the new levels as arguments. For example, the command:

```
umask 077
```

sets the file creation mask for full read and write permission (and execute for directories) for the user, with no permissions for the group and other levels.

The **umask** command should be placed in the ".profile" or ".login" file of any user who is not to assume the default system values.

Changing File Permissions with **chmod**

The **chmod** (change mode) command allows the owner of a file or the superuser to change the permissions of files and directories. The permissions are generally called the *mode* of the file or directory, hence the *change mode* command name. **chmod** allows you to set the access rights of others than the superuser.

The **chmod** command can be used in two modes. The first uses numbers to indicate the access required, and is called *absolute mode*. The second mode uses letters and operators, and is called *symbolic mode*.

Symbolic mode is the most commonly used. In symbolic mode, the **chmod** command has the formats:

```
chmod who - permissions file
chmod who + permissions file
chmod who = permissions file
```

where "who" indicates the users the command will affect. Wildcards are supported for the file names.

The "who" argument of the **chmod** command uses one or more of the letters shown in Table 11.4.

*Table 11.4: **chmod** Commands for "who" Argument*

Command	Description
a	All users (this is the default if nothing is specified)
g	All users in the same group as the owner
o	All users on the system (stands for "others")
u	Owner (or user) of the file or directory

The letter indicating which users will have their access permissions changed is followed by one of: the plus sign, minus sign, or equal sign. The plus sign adds the permissions indicated to the file or directory, regardless of existing permissions, while the minus sign removes the indicated permissions. The equal sign assigns the indicated permissions and removes any not specified.

Possible permissions for a file or directory are shown in Table 11.5.

Table 11.5: File or Directory Permissions

Permission	Description
x	execute (search for directories)
r	read
w	write
l	mandatory file locking during access

There are two other possible permissions, but these not commonly used. The mandatory file locking permission refers to the file having its read and write permissions locked when a program accesses the file, so that more than one user cannot access the file at the same time. A locked file cannot have group execute permission.

Using symbolic mode, the command:

```
$chmod +x file
```

sets "file" to execute permission for all users (the default "a" type is assumed). The command:

```
$chmod go-rw file
```

removes read and write permission for group and others. Finally, the command:

```
$chmod g=rw file
```

sets read and write permissions only for the group.

The **chmod** command supports wildcards, so an entire directory's contents can be changed at once, if necessary. If the files in a directory all had the permissions:

```
-rw-r--r--
```

and a user wished to prevent others from even looking at the files (by removing read permission), the command would be:

```
$chmod go-r *
```

A check of the file list would then show them all to have the following permissions:

```
-rw-------
```

The **chmod** command is often used to make a program executable for all users. The easiest format for this is to issue the command

```
$chmod ugo+rwx file name
```

which grants everyone on the system full access to execute, read, and write the "filename" program. The write permission is often not included, as it is unlikely a user will want to modify the executable file.

The format for **chmod** in absolute mode is:

```
$chmod mode file
```

The mode is arrived at by adding the relevant numbers from the following list:

- 0000   no permission
- 0001   execute by others (search in directories)
- 0002   write by others
- 0004   read by others
- 0010   execute by group (search in directories)
- 0020   write by group
- 0040   read by groups
- 0100   execute by owner (search in directories)
- 0200   write by owner
- 0400   read by owner

For example, the command

```
$chmod 0777 file
```

sets "file" to allow all users to read, write and execute. This is derived by adding the numbers for execute, write and read permission for each of the three categories (owner, group, and other). The command

```
chmod 0600 file
```

will set the permissions to read and write for the owner only.

Changing Owners and Groups

You can change the owner of a file with the **chown** (change owner) command. The name of the new owner must be valid because the system checks it against the list of system users. The command's format is:

```
chown   username   file name
```

where "username" is the new owner of the file and "filename" is the name of the file to be changed. Wildcards are fully supported.

You can change the group affiliation of a file in a similar manner with the **chgrp** (change group) command, using a valid group ID:

```
chgrp   groupID   filename
```

Again, you can use wildcards to change a number of files at once.

Backups

The importance of backups of data cannot be overstressed for multiuser systems. Damage to file systems and data can occur from several sources, including hardware failures, power interruptions, and simple user errors. A backup is a copy of the data in a file system stored on another medium, which can be used to recreate the original. Usually, this medium is tape, but floppy disks or removable hard disks can also be used.

The regular creation of backups is a bother, in many cases. However, the importance of the process is immediately obvious the first time the system crashes or a user needs to recover a file from the backups.

Sources of Damage

UNIX has been in constant use for many years, and its behavior is well known. The very nature of an operating system that provides multiuser and multitasking support means that at any given time, several system files are open, and data may be in the process of being written to (or read from) the hard disk even if no users are logged in. In addition, UNIX maintains a number of tables of information about file systems, both in memory and on disk, which are constantly open, or not cleanly written to the disk in a final format.

Whenever CPU processes are interrupted, system files and tables can be lost from memory, and the disk files that correspond to this information left in a temporary state. The data that these files comprise may be incorrectly written to disk, and may not have proper file identifiers and terminators.

Damage to a file system can occur from a number of sources, few of which are under the control of the system administrators. It is that person's task, however, to take all steps necessary to minimize any potential damage.

Most modern computer power supplies are designed to tolerate a range of voltage or current fluctuations, including those normally found in city supply lines. However, in even the best powerline design, power failures and voltage or current fluctuations are unavoidable.

As a source of damage, power failures are spontaneous and uncontrollable. Although there are uninterruptable power supplies (UPS), which switch in and power computer systems when their regular line sources fail, these devices are expensive and may not react fast enough to a power failure to prevent the system from failing. When a system fails, it is called a *system crash*.

In addition, UPSs tend to provide only a short amount of emergency power, and are intended to give the system administrator just enough time to cleanly shut the system down. If no one is available to do a shutdown, the UPS will eventually power down itself, causing a system crash.

Other power-line problems include voltage spikes, surges, and drops in the power voltage or current (brownouts). Spikes and surges can be minimized with spike protectors, which essentially filter the incoming voltage. Any sudden surges in power are trimmed by the spike filter to a manageable level. Every UNIX system should have a spike filter system in place, as voltage spikes are common enough to cause problems.

Unfortunately, a lot of devices are on the market that claim to be spike filters, but really only perform a minimal job. A power bar with spike protection is usually a limiting device with a fuse circuit. If the fuse blows, the system crashes anyway from power failure. A reputable electrical company will be able to recommend suitable protection for the computer system if provided with the electrical tolerances of the devices and the amount of current the system requires.

It is also beginning to become common practice to place all computing devices, even those from the smallest UNIX implementations, on dedicated power circuits. This way they do not share the same power circuit as the rest of the building. This allows an isolated power supply to feed the computer system, unaffected by sudden power drains in the regular circuits. These drains or sudden power drops can occur when devices such as old photocopy machines are switched on.

Large UNIX systems invariably have isolated power circuits (sometimes separate circuits for the CPU and disk drives themselves), and power *conditioners* to monitor and correct any linesource variations. These devices typically also provide UPS capabilities, but can cost tens of thousands of dollars.

Hardware failures are another common source of failure. Hard disks, for example, are constantly in use, and eventually they will catch up with the best *mean time between failure* figures (MTBF). Hard disk technology has improved consistently over the years, and in general, the MTBF is increasing, but UNIX is a very disk-intensive operating system, and each system will experience a hard disk crash at some time.

Failure of the CPU, support chips, or devices can all cause system crashes, too. Any process that renders the CPU, hard disk, or controlling circuits unable to complete a disk file operation can have disastrous consequences.

Finally, users are a vital reason for backups. Many users will arbitrarily erase files they didn't intend to, or manage to damage a file in some way, and then turn to the system administrator to reconstruct a copy of the file.

Backup Media

The most commonly used medium for backups is tape. Large systems tend to use reels of tape, whereas smaller systems use tape cartridges. Both provide a convenient, high-density storage capacity.

Alternative media include removable hard disks of many different types. These are full hard disks or disk-platter systems, which can be fully removed from the system and stored elsewhere. Several of these disk "packs" can then be cycled on one controller.

The advent of CD (compact disk) and WORM (write once, read many) technologies has also provided a new format for archival storage. As these new systems mature, high capacity fast-access systems will become available.

The floppy disk is a last resort backup device for large file systems, although it is ideal for small files or groups of files. Backing up many megabytes on low capacity floppies is both frustrating and time consuming, so floppies tend not to be used whenever an alternative is available.

The Backup Schedule

UNIX systems are multiuser by their very nature and tend to be in constant use. Unless the system has only a few users, who access the system infrequently, daily backups are essential to avoid future problems.

Many system administrators prefer to perform backups during the early hours of the morning, when few users will be logged in. The exact backup time can be set to minimize impact on any other background processing tasks the system may execute at night. With an automated backup process, the system administrator's responsibility is merely to ensure that the backup was performed properly, check any errors, and change the backup media.

It is foolhardy to keep only one backup copy of a system. Ideally, backups should be kept for days, or even weeks. Backup routines vary, depending on the system administrator, but a comprehensive backup system requires at least two weeks of daily backups.

The most common backup schedule requires between ten and fourteen tapes, depending on whether backups are performed on weekends. All backup tapes should be labeled with names, such as "daily1" through "daily14". These tapes are cycled through, one after another, and the cycle is restarted after all the tapes have been used. This provides a two week queue of backups, allowing retrieval of files for that amount of time. If more tapes are available, they are simply added to the cycle, lengthening the cycle time. Backup tapes should be stored away from the main machine, out of direct sunlight, and away from magnetic sources. Ideally, you should use a fire-proof or fire- retardant storage cabinet.

A daily and weekly backup cycle can be more useful. If, for example, fourteen tapes are available, ten are dedicated to a daily cycle. These can be called "daily1" through "daily10". The four remaining tapes are used for a two week cycle, and are called "week1" through "week4".

With this backup system, you back up with the ten daily tapes and then use the next weekly tape in the sequence. Then you cycle through the daily tapes again, followed by the next weekly tape. The system can be shown as follows:

```
Daily1->Daily10, Week1, Daily1->Daily10, Week2, etc...
```

This has two major advantages. First, when the entire cycle is underway, there are the ten daily backups, which cover a two week period if weekends are not active in the backup cycle. But there are also the two week tapes, which extend back over four daily cycles, or eight weeks. With this system, a file or group of files may be recovered after two months!

The capability to move back an extended period on a backup (in this case two months), provides a means of recovering from undetected errors over the shorter daily cycle. Suppose a file was inadvertently truncated, but that this was not noticed for three weeks. Under the normal daily cycle, this file could not be restored, but with the biweekly backups, there is a good chance of recovery (assuming the file in question wasn't created and damaged during the two-week period between two week tapes, of course).

Tapes should be kept in several locations, if possible. At least one recent tape should be kept either in a fireproof (and nonmagnetic) safe or storage cabinet, or in another physical location entirely. The latter are called *off-site* backups. These off-site backups should be rotated regularly, in case of fire or other disaster that might destroy the backup tapes themselves.

If more tapes are available, either the daily or two week cycle can be extended. It is also a good idea to have dedicated tapes for offsite backups in this cycle, fitting in after the two week tapes, for example. This backup cycle can be modified at will. Many system administrators prefer to keep monthly tapes as well.

It is not always necessary to back up all the files on a system every night, especially if this would mean breaking the backup over several tapes. Instead, you can perform a full backup at intervals (the system files will not change much, if at all), and backup the directories that store user files and application data files daily. If the system has been carefully set up, this can be accomplished with one recursive directory backup. It is typical to make a backup of the "/usr" (or "/u" directory, if one exists) daily, but leave the rest for full backups.

The Backup Log

A key element of any backup schedule is keeping a log of the backups. The backup log should be updated whenever a backup is completed, and kept for reference. A typical backup log includes the following:

- date of backup
- name of backup tape
- UNIX volume being backed up (e.g., /dev0)
- whether a full or partial backup was performed—if partial, directories backed up
- who made the backup and cycled the tape
- whether the backup was automatic or manual
- storage location (if different than default)

This information will help the system administrator should it become necessary to restore files. The backup dates obviously help keep track of when the last backup was performed and also act as an index. If a file was deleted by accident three days ago, the proper backup tape for the file restore can be determined from the log dates.

Volume names are important if more than one volume is maintained on a system. If a single volume is used, this is not necessary. Tracking full or partial backups is relevant when only certain subdirectories are used for the nightly backup. When system files are not backed up daily, it is necessary to know which tape holds a full system image in case a full system restore is needed.

Many system administrators track whether the backup was performed automatically (for example, by **cron**), or whether it was done manually by a user. While this may not have any direct significance, it will help if **cron** has failed repeatedly or some other system defect has corrupted the nightly automatic backups. The manual backups are sometimes referred to as "unscheduled" backups. Also, the storage location can be noted if it is not a regular place. A code can indicate whether the backup is off-site, or in a fireproof location, for example.

A system backup log can be made easily by using a word processor to create a blank form consisting of the columns for data required, and line-by-line entry for each backup. A typical page, with ruled lines between entries, can then hold several weeks' worth of data.

The backup log should be maintained near the system, for convenience, or near the location of the backup storage. Some system administrators keep a duplicate copy of the backup log in another site, with an off-site copy or in a fireproof location.

The backup Account

Many UNIX versions provide a special account for backups, called **backup**. Most users cannot perform full backups and restores because of permissions, and the superuser's account has unrestricted permission, which may damage or alter permissions on some files. The special **backup** account is a restricted "root" account. It usually invokes a shell program that helps create backups and restore files quickly. The password for **backup** is set when the system is installed, and can be the same as the superuser password.

Not all UNIX versions have the **backup** account, but for those that do not, you can create one. The **umask** setting should allow **backup** to access all the files that must be routinely saved to backup media.

When a **backup** account is supplied with the operating system, it may include an automated backup sequence. This would be described in the system administrator's guide.

Using tar for Backups

The **tar** (tape archiver) program is used to save files and directories to an archive medium, usually tape or disk, and restore them back. The format of the command is:

```
tar switch modifiers files
```

The switch and modifier arguments are explained below. The file, files, or directories that you want to archive or restore are the last items on the command line.

Only one switch is used with **tar** at a time. Valid switches are shown in Table 11.6.

*Table 11.6: Valid **tar** Switches*

Switch	Description
r	write to end of existing archive
x	extract from the archive (recursive)
t	list names of files in archives as they occur
u	files added if not modified or archived already
c	create a new archive media

In addition, you can add a series of modifiers to the **tar** command switch to control the format of the archive. Valid modifiers are listed in Table 11.7.

Default values for most **tar** functions are stored in a file usually called "etc/default/tar", and are used unless specifically overridden with the **tar** command switches.

*Table 11.7: Valid **tar** Modifiers*

Modifier	Description
0-7	specifies the drive to be archived
A	suppresses absolute filenames
b	provides a blocking factor of 1-20 (tape only)
e	prevents splitting files across volumes
f	gives the archive media device name
F	gives the name of a file for **tar** arguments
k	gives size of archive volume in kilobytes
l	displays error messages if links unresolved
m	does not restore modification times
n	indicates the archive is not a tape
p	extracts files with their original permissions
v	verbose output (lists files on the console)
w	displays archive action and waits for user confirmation

The **tar** command uses absolute pathnames, unless the "A" switch is specified. If you archive the file "/usr/tim/foobar" when in the root directory, and then restore it when in the "/usr/tmp" directory, the file is restored correctly to "/usr/tim". However, relative pathnames can be used, so if you archived the file "./foobar" when logged in to "/usr/tim", then switch to "/usr/tmp" and extract the file suppressing absolute filenames, it will now be in "/usr/tmp/foobar". The period before the slash indicates a relative pathname. Absolute pathnames are always relative to the root directory, while relative pathnames are relative to the current working directory.

A few examples will help explain the switches. If you are using a tape drive designated "/dev/rct0", and the files that are to be archived total less than the tape's capacity, the archive can be created with the command:

```
#tar cf /dev/rct0 /
```

The device name is specified by the "f" option, and "/" indicates you want to archive the entire root directory system. The "c" option indicates this is a new archive, and any old files on the tape will be overwritten. If the "v" option had been included in the switches, the filenames and sizes would be echoed to the screen as they are archived.

To restore the entire file system from the tape created in the above example, the command is:

    #tar xf /dev/rct0

This restores all files, as the default is the entire tape. To restore a single file from the tape, the command is:

    #tar xf /dev/rct0 file

This uses an absolute pathname for the file, as the "A" option was not used.

You can display the list of files on a tape with the command

    #tar tvf /dev/rct0

This uses the "v" option to display the results from **tar**. Many system administrators redirect this command to a file and print it out, to save a hard copy of the tape's contents for future reference.

Tapes usually require a blocking factor when creating an archive, but **tar** can read this from the tape when extracting files. When archiving to a tape, the blocking factor is specified with the "b" modifier.

When a tape is not large enough to hold the entire archive, more than one tape is needed. This requires using the "k" option to specify the archive's size. The command:

    #tar cvbfk 20 /dev/rct0 122880 /

tells **tar** to use a blocking factor of "20", device "/dev/rct0", and a tape capacity of 122880 kilobytes (approx 120 MB). The order of the arguments is decided by the order in which the switches are specified.

When floppy disks are used, archives usually require more than one disk, and the "k" option is used to specify the archive volumes capacity. To back up the root directory system to 1.2 Mb diskettes, the command is:

    tar cnfk /dev/fd1 1200 /

In this example, "/dev/fd1" is the name of the floppy drive and "1200" is the size of the disk in kilobytes. The "n" modifier tells **tar** that this is not a tape, and **tar** will run a little more efficiently than if the modifier had been left off.

It is sometimes necessary to provide the full device name, such as "/dev/rfd096ds15", for floppy disks and other backup media, depending on the version of UNIX you are using.

Process Accounting

UNIX provides the system administrator with the ability to enable a process accounting system using built-in UNIX commands. Process accounting allows the system to track the amount of time each user spends logged in. It also tracks the number of processes started by each user, the amount of time each process used, and details about the size and system requirements of the processes.

Process accounting is not required for many systems, but if a user is charged for connect time, or system time, it provides a simple method of determining the user's charges. Even when the user is not charged, process accounting allows the system administrator to measure the amount of use each user puts on the system, and to identify heavy users and programs.

Process accounting does increase the amount of overhead on the system: When it is active, it must track the processes and write the information to a file. This overhead is not considerable, but on heavily used systems it can be detrimental to performance. The process accounting file sizes should be monitored carefully to avoid wasting too much disk space.

Starting and Stopping Process Accounting

You activate process accounting with the **accton** command, which can be embedded in the UNIX system startup file "/etc/rc". You supply the name of the process accounting file where information is to be stored, as an argument to the **accton** command. By convention, this is usually called "/usr/adm/pacct":

```
#accton /usr/adm/pacct
```

When the command is executed, any existing information in the file is deleted, and a new process accounting system is started with an empty file. If the file does not exist, it is created.

Because the command deletes any old information, it is necessary to copy the existing information from the file first if you wish to archive or print it. Although system administrators will print out the information regularly in case of a system crash, it is wise to copy the old file first with instructions in the "/etc/rc" file:

```
mv /usr/adm/pacct /usr/adm/oldpacct
accton /usr/adm/pacct
```

and then print or archive the old copy before the entire process is repeated with another system restart.

Many "/etc/rc" files have the process accounting information already in them, but commented out with the "#" character. In this case, a system administrator simply needs to remove the comment symbols to activate the process accounting lines at the next system start.

The easiest way to stop process accounting is to comment out the lines in the "/etc/rc" file and restart the system.

Accessing Process Accounting Information

The process accounting information saved by the **accton** command can be read and displayed by a program called **acctcom**. Depending on the arguments to the command, a variety of information can be displayed. Usually, **acctcom** lists the command executed, user name, terminal ID, start and end times, real process time on system, actual CPU seconds, mean size in kilo bytes, any forks, and system exit status.

You issue the **acctcom** command with a file name for the process accounting file as an argument. If you do not supply one, it displays "/usr/adm/pacct", the default. Several useful options are provided, including the ability to read information backwards (latest entries first) with **-b**. The **-h** option, which displays the fraction of total CPU time used by a process, enables you to identify processes that "hog" the CPU.

Chapter 12

Peripherals and Devices

UNIX treats every peripheral attached to the hardware as a file. Hard disks are files, terminals are files, and printers are files. To be more precise, each of these peripherals is described in a file that tells UNIX how to communicate with that peripheral. (This is something of a simplification, but a useful one at this time.)

Each peripheral attached to the system is called a *device* in UNIX terminology. The files that describe these peripherals or devices are called *device files*.

Throughout the following discussion of devices, you must bear in mind that each version of UNIX can be slightly different. Although the principles remain the same, the exact means of dealing with devices depends on the version. For illustration purposes, we will assume a combination of PC-based UNIX and XENIX software implementations, which serve as good examples for UNIX versions from PCs to supercomputers.

Device Files and Numbers

The device files are divided into two types, depending on how information is passed from the device to the kernel. The kernel is the portion of the operating system that loads during the boot process and controls the entire UNIX system. While it does not contain the entire operating system itself, the kernel has instructions for reading in the parts it needs from a disk drive when required.

A block mode device transfers data between itself and UNIX in fixed-size blocks, usually the same size as the sector size. Typical block mode devices are hard disks and tapes, where transferring the data in complete blocks is much more efficient than the other method.

The second type of device is a character mode device. These devices do not use fixed-size chunks for data transfer, but can change the amount of information transferred dynamically. Usually they transfer a single character at a time. Examples of character mode devices are terminals and modems.

Block mode devices use sections of RAM to transfer the blocks of data. These RAM sections are called buffers, although buffers can also reside on disk drives and in the hardware's architecture itself. Character mode devices do not normally use buffers. Instead, data is transferred directly between the system and the device. Those character devices that transfer data directly are also called *raw devices*.

All devices on the UNIX system are assigned some mnemonic code to identify them to the system and the users. The first hard disk, for example, is called **hd0** (the zero identifies it as the first hard disk). A second hard disk would be **hd1**. Floppy disks are usually identified by specifying the physical layout of the disk.

A 1.2 Mb capacity floppy has 96 tracks per inch and 15 sectors per track, and is usually called **fd096ds15**. The "fd" refers to "floppy disk" and the "ds" to "disk sectors", the number of sectors per track on the disk. A typical 360 Kb floppy is called **fd048ds9**, as it has 48 tracks per inch and 9 sectors per track.

A tape drive uses the mnemonic for magnetic tape, and is called **mt0** if it is the first tape drive on the system. Some systems use the shortened form for cartridge tape, **ct0**.

In many cases, it can be shown that a device is a raw device by preceding the name with the letter "r". The magnetic tape drive just mentioned, addressed in a raw mode, would be called **rmt0**.

To show that all these files represent devices, the files are stored in a directory called "dev", and so a hard disk is properly defined as "/dev/hd0", a tape as "/dev/mt0", and so on. When these names are used, UNIX knows to look for information about the device in the "/dev" directory. (The "/dev" directory is used by convention, but any other subdirectory could be used as easily.)

So that UNIX can identify different devices, it assigns two numbers to each device. The first number is called the major number, and indicates what kind of device driver is used to communicate with the device. (The driver is a set of instructions.) The second number is called the minor number, and uniquely identifies the device. No two devices have the same combination of major and minor numbers.

It is easy to see the use of these numbers in the naming of terminals. Most terminals can be talked to by the same method, and so they all use the same device driver. But to know which terminal to talk to, UNIX gives each terminal a different number.

How UNIX Uses a Terminal

A UNIX system, when started, attempts to establish communications with the peripherals attached to it. UNIX knows which terminals should be present and connected (but not necessarily switched on) by reading a file (usually) called "/etc/ttys". The layout of "/etc/ttys" is simple, and a section of a typical file might look like this:

```
1mtty01
1mtty02
1mtty03
0mtty04
0mtty05
...
```

```
1Etty80
1Etty81
1Etty82
0Etty83
...
```

The file consists of a long list of the different *ports* (devices) available to the system. Each port is a prospective terminal, printer, modem, or other character mode device. Each line of the file tells three important pieces of information.

The first character of each line tells whether that device is active, or enabled. A "1" indicates it is enabled, while a "0" indicates it is disabled. If a device is active, UNIX runs processes to allow communications with that device. (The word active here does not mean switched on or in use, but rather it refers to whether the device is connected and recognized as such by UNIX.)

The second character tells UNIX what communications parameters to use with that device. The second character can be a letter or number, and it refers to an entry in a file, usually called "/etc/gettydefs". The "gettydefs" file has a column of numbers or letters, one of which matches the character in the second column of the "ttys" file, followed by information on the baud rate, number of bits, and more. (We will discuss the "gettydefs" file in more detail in the next section.)

The remaining characters of the "ttys" file identify the terminal or printer identification. Each device attached to UNIX has a major and minor number. Each device also has a short-form name. Character mode devices, such as terminals, serial printers, and modems, are referred to as "tty" devices if they are on serial ports. Each port has a unique designation, such as "tty01", "tty02", and so on. The port numbers can vary considerably, depending on the UNIX version and the hardware. Multiport cards use port numbers like "tty81", "tty82", etc., or "tty4a", "tty4b". When a multiport card is installed, the board's installation software usually enters the proper port numbers into the "/etc/ttys" file.

If a terminal is enabled, UNIX starts a background process called "getty" that allows the terminal to communicate with the operating system. All enabled terminals have a corresponding "getty" on the system, which can be seen with the **ps** command. The process reads the "/etc/gettydefs" entry and sets the baud rate and communications parameters for that port. Each terminal usually has a **login** process active for the terminal to allow users to log in.

A terminal without a user on it will not "talk back" to the operating system, but the system monitors the enabled terminal lines to watch for any activity. When someone logs in at a terminal, another file, called "/etc/ttytype" can be read. This file contains a list of the default terminal types for each port. Although this can be overridden by a user's ".profile" or ".login" file, the terminal type in "/etc/ttytype" allows the operating system to assume it knows the type of terminal it is connected to. For hardwired terminals, this frees the user from worrying about terminal types.

The "gettydefs" File

The "/etc/gettydefs" file contains a list of the most commonly used communications parameters. Each set of parameters is identified by either a number or a letter. The data following the letter or number tells UNIX the baud rate at which the device communicates, how many bits to use, whether parity is used, and other information about the terminal's expected behavior.

When a terminal is enabled, the system accesses this file to determine what parameters to use. The correct entry is defined by the second character of the line entry for each port in the file "/etc/ttys".

The "/etc/gettydefs" file also allows a system administrator to change the login prompt that appears on the screen and to control a cascade through a number of different parameter lines to determine baud rates. Modems, for example, may run up to 9600 baud, but a user calling in on a modem line may have only 2400 baud. It is necessary for the UNIX system to determine the baud rate by matching a set of the entries in "/etc/gettydefs" to the baud rate it detects.

Entries in the "/etc/gettydefs" file can be edited and added to, but it is wise to do this carefully. Your UNIX documentation will fully explain the meaning of the different options that can be placed in a parameter list.

Adding a Terminal

The most common device on a UNIX system is a terminal. These terminals come in a wide variety of models, from bare bones to very elaborate. Each terminal, though, talks to the UNIX system in a fairly consistent manner. Terminals are invariably serial devices, that is, they send information to and from UNIX one character at a time. They are character mode devices.

Terminals are usually connected to the UNIX system through an RS-232 port. These may have nine-pin or the more common twenty-five-pin connectors. Some UNIX systems have add-on boards with banks of serial connectors for character devices like terminals and printers.

Assuming, for the moment, that cables are wired correctly, the steps in connecting a new terminal to the UNIX system are:

1. Identify the terminal type
2. Set the communications parameters
3. Connect the cables
4. Enable the terminal

These steps may be made more or less complicated by the hardware you are using.

The terminal type is determined from the "/etc/termcap" file. Most terminals are identified in this file either by their full names or by mnemonics. The terminal's manual should identify the full name of the terminal type, such as "Qume QVT 119+" or "Wyse 60", and provide a list of any emulations the terminal supports. (Emulations modify a terminal's codes to match those of another terminal.)

Terminals that are not included in the "/etc/termcap" file may have an emulation mode that is already entered. If neither the terminal nor its emulations (if any) are in the file, then you must make a special entry that describes the terminal to the UNIX system. Full details on adding to the "termcap" file can be found in the various UNIX implementation guides.

It is unusual to encounter a terminal that does not exist in "etc/termcap", though. These files have been built up over the years to include almost every known terminal that has appeared, so unless the terminal is brand new, it is probably embedded in the file somewhere. You can use the **more** command and the search option (triggered with "/") to scan the file for any variations on the terminal name.

Once you identify the terminal type in "/etc/termcap", you must note the short-form mnemonic. Many system administrators enter the default name of the terminal in the "/etc/ttytype" file and eliminate the terminal type question from user login routines. Instead, each ".profile" or ".login" command file has the entry:

    tset -r

in it, which uses the default terminal type specified in "/etc/ttytype" and preempts asking the user for the terminal type.

The parameters the terminal is set for should be noted. This includes the number of bits it uses, the type of parity (if used), the baud rate, handshaking, and more. This data is then compared with the communications parameters in the "/etc/gettydefs" file and, when a matching entry is found, it is entered in the "/etc/ttys" file next to the port number of the new terminal.

In some cases, the terminal's parameters are best altered to suit a standard entry in the "/etc/gettydefs" file. Many system administrators try to have all hardwired terminals use the same "gettydefs" entry for convenience. This may require using the terminal's setup capabilities to adjust the communications parameters.

When you have determined the terminal type and have entered the communications parameters in the "etc/ttys" file, you attach the cable and enable the terminal. To enable the terminal, enter:

```
#enable ttyxx
```

where "ttyxx" is the port name. UNIX then begins a "getty" process and a **login** process for the port, and attempts to set up the requested communications parameters with the terminal. If all goes well, a login prompt should appear on the terminal in a few seconds.

Troubleshooting

If a prompt is not received on the terminal but some garbled letters do appear, then the terminal's communications parameters are not set to coincide with the entry in "/etc/gettydefs". These should be checked. Usually, the baud rate is incorrect.

If nothing is shown on the terminal, the most probable cause of error is the cable. Some terminals must be wired with a straight-through cable (all pins connected to their opposite number on the other end of the cable), while some need a null- modem cable (some pins crossed within the cabling). This depends on the type of multiport board used (if one is being used), or the terminal's type. Check the manuals for the ports and the terminal wiring.

The system administrator can use a **ps** command to make sure that UNIX started a **getty** for the new terminal:

```
#ps -t ttyxx
```

where "ttyxx" is the port name for the terminal. If one is started, an entry similar to the following is displayed:

```
  PID  TTY  TIME COMMAND
16836   82  0:00 getty
```

this indicates that **getty** is active for that terminal. If a **getty** is not listed, the port is not enabled correctly.

To disconnect a terminal, disable the port with the command:

    #disable ttyxx

where "ttyxx" is the port name. This cancels any **getty** and **login** processes running for that port, and marks it as disabled in the "/etc/ttys" file.

Adding a Modem

Modems are treated in exactly the same way as terminals, but they use a different line in the "/etc/gettydefs" file. Port names can be slightly different for modems. If the modem is not to be controlled by UNIX, the port name is the same as a terminal, but if modem control is required, a slightly different name is used. Sometimes the port name for a modem differs from that for a nonmodem only in that the identifying letter is uppercase. Other times, a modem requires a different port number.

In some cases, a "tty8a" port does not involve modem control, whereas "tty8A" does. Alternatively, with some multiport boards, "tty8a" does not have modem control, whereas "tty9a" does. This must be determined from the multiport board documentation.

Most modems work quite well without modem control. The addition of the modem control allows the UNIX system to completely control most functions of the modem, including hanging it up and detecting various modem status signals.

Printers

UNIX supports both parallel and serial printers, and there may be more than one of each type on a system. In order to control printing, UNIX uses a series of programs that install, buffer, and monitor printer behavior.

UNIX assigns one printer as a default printer, to be used unless another printer is specified. UNIX is versatile with respect to printers: Many types can be used simultaneously, including local printers (attached to terminals) and remote printers (attached by modems).

The UNIX command set that controls the printer environment is basic to the operating system, although several variations are available commercially or with some licensed UNIX vendors. The system described here is the basic UNIX command system.

All printers on a UNIX system are assigned a name. Usually, this name is descriptive, such as "laser" for a laser printer. The printer name can be up to fourteen characters long.

A system administrator with many printers can group them into different classes. Then, when a print request is sent to a particular class, the first available printer performs the request. This is especially useful for heavy printer sites, where a bank of printers is needed to keep up with the demand.

Connecting a Printer

A parallel printer is easy to attach; it is simply connected to one of the parallel ports on the system using a standard Centronics cable. The port number must be known. Most machines designate parallel ports as "lp0", "lp1", and so on. The hardware manuals should provide this information. If not, it becomes a matter of trial and error to determine the correct port number. (Some systems tell you what parallel ports are present when the system is booted. Watch the diagnostic messages to see if this occurs.)

Serial printers are connected either through a main serial port, or through a multiport expansion card. Serial printers should be set up to employ either XON/XOFF or DTR protocols. Both XON/XOFF and DTR are communications methods between the printer and UNIX that tell UNIX when the printer is ready to accept data and when it is busy. By using these, the printer does not lose any information.

The port the printer is attached to must be disabled before it is connected. The serial communications parameters must be set correctly, otherwise the printer will not function properly. Ensure that the baud rate, number of bits, parity, and protocol are all set at both the printer end and in the UNIX configuration. Parallel printers do not need all of this, as the parallel port definition includes many of the parameters preset to default values. When a parallel port is selected, both the printer and UNIX know how to communicate without the system administrator defining the details.

After connecting the printer, you can test it quickly by trying to route something to the device with redirection. For example, you can enter:

    #date > /dev/lpname

where "lpname" is the name of the printer port device. If the port is correct, the printer prints the output of the **date** command. If nothing happens, either the port is incorrectly set up, or there is a hardware fault.

The printer is connected to most UNIX systems using the **mkdev lp** command. This command provides a series of questions about the printer's type (parallel or serial), the port, the printer's name, the interface program to be used, and whether this is the default system printer. (Some UNIX versions may ask different questions or use a menu system, but the information required is basically the same.)

The interface program contains the commands that cause the printer to execute print instructions properly. For example, some laser printers may require particular setup strings for the different print modes they support. Most printers for UNIX are straightforward devices that require no special instructions. These use the "dumb" interface default that UNIX offers. Some printers, or adventurous system administrators who wish to optimize their system, may use other interfaces that provide expanded capabilities. This is especially true with text-formatting systems.

The Print Spooler

The UNIX print spooler allows printer requests to be queued for printing. This prevents conflicts when more than one user tries to print at the same time and also allows some prioritization of printer requests. Additionally, the items in the print queue can be moved to other printers, deleted, or held. The default print spooler with UNIX is called **lp** (for line printer).

When a printer request is sent, UNIX assigns a "request ID" to the request. Each time something is sent to the printer, UNIX assigns the printout to a file, and lets the spooler (print controller) handle when it is physically sent to the printer. An image of the printout is saved in the spooler's file area. Each printout is assigned a unique number, consisting of the printer's name and a number, such as "laser-10" or "daisy-198". This number is called the *print request ID*, and refers back to the image of the file to be printed.

UNIX provides a background print spooler program called **lpsched**, which is started when UNIX is initialized. This program is responsible for routing all printer requests through the proper interface, and then to the printer port. The **lpsched** program must be stopped by the system administrator whenever modifications to the printer definitions must be made.

You can monitor the condition of the spooler by using the command **lpstat -r**. This returns a single line that indicates whether the spooler is running or not. The **lpstat** command can also provide much more information about printer status and printer queues, and we will discuss this in more detail shortly.

The spooler can be started up or shut down by a system administrator with the **lpsched** and **lpshut** commands, respectively. It is often necessary to indicate the full path of these commands:

```
#/usr/lib/lpsched
#/usr/lib/lpshut
```

if the PATH variable does not include "/usr/lib" (by default it does not).

Every time a printer request is sent, **lpsched** adds an entry to a "/usr/spool/lp/log" file that includes the printer request ID, user, printer sent to, date and time. This file is reset whenever the system is rebooted or **lpsched** is restarted. The old file is saved as "/usr/spool/lp/oldlog", and a new "log" file created. If any errors occur during a printer request, they are recorded in the log files.

Controlling the Spooler

UNIX provides the capability to move printer requests between printers or to cancel them entirely. You can determine the status of all printers and the print spooler queue at any time with a single command.

The status of the printers can be determined with the **lpstat** command. If **lpstat** is issued with no arguments, it lists all the requests the user currently has in the spooler. The **lpstat -r** option prints the status of the spooler, while **lpstat -t** prints all status information. This latter format is very useful for a system administrator.

You use the **lpmove** command to move a printer request from one printer to another. To use this, you must first stop the scheduler. You can indicate a global move of all requests or a single request by its ID for a specific printer. For example, the file "laser-123" can be moved from the printer "laser" to "daisy" with the commands:

```
#/usr/lib/lpshut
#/usr/lib/lpmove laser-123 daisy
#/usr/lib/lpsched
```

The full pathnames are specified in these examples because the "usr/lib" directory is not usually in the default path. Of course, the path could be modified to include this directory. As you can see, you must stop the spooler before these commands and start it again after them. To move all requests from "laser" to "daisy", the command becomes:

```
#/usr/lib/lpshut
#/usr/lib/lpmove laser daisy
#/usr/lib/lpsched
```

and the "laser" device then has no requests queued.

All requests for printing on a specific printer can be prevented using the **reject** command. To prevent any more requests going to the "daisy" printer, for example, you would use the command:

    #/usr/lib/reject daisy

This prevents any requests from being accepted. Any print requests waiting though, remain, as long as the printer is enabled.

A diagnostic message can be echoed back to the user, if required, by adding it to the command:

    #/usr/lib/reject -r"laser down for servicing" laser

where the printer name is supplied last, and the **-r** option enables the message. You can put a space after the "-r", if desired, but one is not necessary. The quotation marks around the message are not printed. If someone tries to send a print request to the "laser" printer after this command is issued, the message:

    lp: cannot accept requests for destination "laser"
    -- printer laser down for servicing

is displayed.

If a printer has been disabled, it must be enabled again before it can be used to print a file. To reenable the printer, first issue the **accept** command and then the **enable** command:

    /usr/lib/accept laser
    enable laser

The **disable** command disables the printer, using the same format as the **enable** command.

A user or the system administrator can cancel a print request if they know the request ID (or can determine it from the **lpstat** command). To cancel the printer file "laser-123", issue the command:

    #cancel laser-123

If the printer has already received the request, but is holding it in a buffer before printing, it cannot be canceled. Only while the request ID is active in the spooler can it be canceled.

A summary of this chapter's commands is shown in Table 12.1.

Table 12.1: Summary of Commands

Command	Description
cancel	cancels a printer request
disable	deactivates a port
enable	activates a port
lp	routes to the printer
lp move	moves a printer request to another printer
lpsched	starts the print spooler
lpshut	stops the print spooler
lpstat	displays print and scheduler status information
reject	prevents requests from going to specified printer

Chapter 13

UNIX Standards and GUIs

For purposes of useful discussion, this book has made several generalizations about UNIX, especially in the chapters on system administration. In fact, however, UNIX is currently available in dozens of versions, some conforming to AT&T's UNIX, and some differing considerably. Hardware manufacturers have licensed UNIX and created their own versions, known by a variety of names. Digital Equipment sells Ultrix, IBM has AIX, Santa Cruz Operation has XENIX, and so on. Each version is slightly different, and implements UNIX functions in different ways.

Defining a Standard UNIX

The number of UNIX versions leads to a considerable amount of confusion and incompatibility of software. Several years ago, it became painfully obvious that somebody had to define a single set of criteria to which all UNIX versions would adhere. AT&T, the originators of UNIX, began this process by releasing a description of its UNIX version under the title, "System V Interface Definition", or SVID. Many hardware manufacturers have modified existing versions or released new versions of their UNIX products to meet SVID.

AT&T also teamed up with several other companies to form a technical group that would set standards for future UNIX systems and applications. This consortium has produced a set of standards compatible with SVID, called the X/Open environment.

The IEEE formed a committee to set about creating another set of standards, called the Portable Operating System Standard, which is generally known as POSIX. POSIX is also SVID compatible, although it differs from X/Open.

Support for BSD UNIX, once a major competitor to AT&T's UNIX, has gradually diminished since the release of SVID. Companies that offer BSD-based versions of UNIX are now beginning to offer both BSD and SVID compatible systems.

GUIs

Throughout the earlier chapters of this book, UNIX is presented as you would see it when you use one of the shells. All the commands, programming basics, and system administration routines are discussed from the point of view of someone using a standard terminal connected to a UNIX system.

While many UNIX installations are still of this nature, there is a trend on smaller UNIX systems toward a newer type of interface that replaces the shell's task of communicating between you and the operating system. These new systems use a graphical interface and pointing devices (such as a *mouse*) to allow you to perform many functions.

These new systems are called *graphical user interfaces*, or GUIs (pronounced "gooey"), and they provide you with several distinct advantages over the basic UNIX terminal. Most GUIs allow *windows* to be created and moved about by the user. More than one window can be on your screen at the same time, either as small windows that sit side by side, on top of each other, or in some way so that the two are completely visible, or they can overlap each other, so that one is partially (or completely) hidden by the one in front of it.

With UNIX, each window usually represents a separate process, so using several windows allows you to do more than one thing at a time, and see them running on the same screen. You can think of windows as a small snapshot of the screen that you would see if you had the process inside that window running on the whole screen. Most GUIs, in fact, allow you to expand one window to cover the entire screen. The windows can be a reduced image of the full screen, or with some GUIs they are a section of the screen, with the rest masked by other windows.

A typical GUI screen has one window surrounded by a box. The window contains either pictures or words that describe different aspects of the UNIX system. For example, you may have a picture of a document, which calls the word processor when you point to it. Or you might have a picture of a file folder with a name underneath it, which represents a file you have created.

With GUIs, pictures represent the programs and files you have access to. In some directories, there are going to be a lot of pictures if there are many files, so using pictures for everything on your system is going to become extremely crowded and somewhat overwhelming! Usually, pictures are used to represent the most important things on your system, such as the major applications. Word processors, databases, spreadsheets, and other programs all have their own pictures. Your home directory probably has a separate picture too. When you select your directory you either get the shell prompt character, or another window opens, listing your files.

GUIs use windows for just about everything they do. When you select one picture in one window, another window opens to expand on the item selected. In some cases, this can cause many windows to be open at one time on the screen. However, you are really only using one window at a time, even though you can switch between several windows on your screen. Because UNIX is multi-tasking, though, each one of your open windows can be running processes.

GUIs offer several advantages. They get rid of the shell, and many users never have to learn very much about UNIX to use a terminal with a GUI.

GUIs are more intuitive then shell commands, and allow you to get a better idea of what is going on with your processes with a quick glance at the windows you have open. GUIs present a friendly, non-threatening environment in which to work, and actually can make you more productive because you can monitor more than one process at a time. Finally, a major advantage to GUIs is that different applications written for a particular GUI present similar images to the user, and work on all equipment that supports that GUI.

Naturally, anything with advantages has drawbacks, too. GUIs require a lot of memory to maintain the windows and processes, as well as the GUI software itself. They need screens capable of supporting high resolution graphics, which means your old terminals just won't work. Also, developing programs for use in a GUI is a lot more work than developing a similar program for use by the shell. Many users who are adept at UNIX also find working through a GUI slower and more restricting than from a shell.

As computer power increases, though, you will find yourself wanting to use more of the capabilities of your equipment. Whether you are using a large mainframe or a microcomputer, using a GUI can help make you more productive.

A Brief GUI History

Xerox's Palo Alto Research Center (PARC) began experimenting with graphic-based interfaces between users, applications and operating systems in the 1970s. The PARC developers used a pointing device to move around the screen, which displayed pictures or symbols of the system. PARC did a considerable amount of work toward refining the use of a graphics-based interface, and served as the starting point for other developers to expand and refine it.

GUIs became commercially popular with the development of the Apple Macintosh. The Macintosh presented a graphics-based interface to the user, hiding the operating system behind simple pictures (called *icons*) and *pull-down menus*. A *mouse* moved a pointer around the screen, minimizing the use of the keyboard. The Macintosh's appeal was based on ease of use and ease of learning. No complicated operating system commands were necessary for any system function.

Microsoft tried to emulate the Macintosh interface for the microcomputer. Microsoft Windows and similar products from other companies provided a Mac-like appearance for DOS. As these interfaces gained in popularity, many commercial applications began to include pull-down and pop-up menus, windows, and mouse capabilities as part of their basic package.

The appeal of these interfaces was quickly recognized, and they moved into the UNIX arena. Workstation manufacturers like Sun and Hewlett-Packard, who used UNIX versions, began to develop GUIs for their machines. The target was simple: windows running several applications at once on a single screen, all controlled by a mouse and simple menus. Larger UNIX vendors began to develop their own GUIs, and the PC market followed suit.

Initially, different software companies developed their own GUI interfaces, which were incompatible with each other. Most of the GUIs were written specifically by hardware companies to run on their own machinery, so UNIX portability was lost, due to the different GUIs. A piece of software written to run under one manufacturer's GUI on one machine would not run on a different manufacturer's machine with a different GUI.

To solve this problem, and return to the UNIX ideal of portable software, hardware and software manufacturers tried to develop a set of standards for GUIs, and the way applications interact with them. As could have been expected, several factions developed, each promoting different standards. A vendor that had spent millions of dollars developing its own GUI was reluctant to throw it all away and adopt someone else's software as a standard.

Most GUIs look similar to each other. They use graphics symbols to represent the different capabilities of the system, and a mouse to move a pointer around the screen. Most GUIs use windows that can overlap, each window representing a different process or application.

Beneath the superficial similarities, though, GUIs differ considerably. Each type of GUI uses a different technique for displaying windows and executing applications. Writing a program to work inside a GUI can be a very convoluted and difficult task, as many GUIs have demanding technical requirements.

One proposal that was adopted by many vendors is called "X Windows". X Windows provides a description of the way in which an application is to interact with the GUI. Each hardware manufacturer was able to write a program that supported X Windows applications on its hardware. In theory, as long as a software company wrote applications to use the X Windows technical specifications, they would run on all hardware that supported X Windows.

X Windows

X Windows was released in 1987 by the Massachusetts Institute of Technology's Project Athena, which attempted to build a complete integrated campus network for MIT. Project Athena involved integrating hardware from many manufacturers through the use of an *open system* standard that included UNIX. (An open system is one that applies to more than one manufacturer, and hence is not proprietary to any one vendor.)

The X Windows system was Project Athena's windowing system interface, and could run on either AT&T or BSD UNIX. X Windows very quickly became an accepted system in the industry, encompassing vendors who had up to that point refused to accept a standard UNIX. One example is Sun Microsystems, who had developed their own interface called Network Window System (NeWS). Following a vigorous debate about the relative merits of NeWS versus X Windows, Sun announced that they would support X Windows within the NeWS environment.

A refinement of the X Windows specification resulted in a better graphical appearance on the screen. This refinement, called "Motif", builds on the X Windows standards to add another layer of specifications. Motif is visually more appealing than X Windows.

Expanding the GUIs

Standards require time to be adopted, as the bureaucracy involved in adopting an industry standard is amazing when many large corporations are involved. For this reason, many manufacturers use a "working standard" (a draft of the proposed standard that has yet to become an "official standard"), and base their systems on that. Enhancements are added, which may become part of a newer standard in the future.

Official standards are usually adopted well after a product has become a de facto standard in common use. The UNIX market is constantly refining itself and changing to meet the needs of customers, and to take advantage of increasing technology and the development of new software.

X Windows, as mentioned earlier, was quickly adopted as a de facto standard, and Motif seems to have followed in its footsteps. GUIs that are based on Motif and X Windows are available for most hardware platforms.

In 1989, the microcomputer saw the development of a GUI that finally provided a comprehensive environment for these smaller machines. The Santa Cruz Operation (SCO) teamed up with several other companies to produce a GUI called Open Desktop that combines a number of industry accepted software products into one package designed for microcomputers.

Open Desktop includes SCO's UNIX version, a graphical interface and manager based on Motif and on X Windows, DOS integration (the ability to run DOS programs within UNIX), a Structured Query Language (SQL) database from Ingres, and the standardized networking products TCP/IP and NFS. All together, Open Desktop provides a very comprehensive set of products in one environment, available at a fraction of the cost of each individual product.

Open Desktop is destined to become a de facto standard for microcomputers based on the Intel 80386 and 80486 CPUs. It has earned the support of a considerable number of software and hardware manufacturers, and presents a solid product. It requires a hefty amount of RAM and hard disk space, but provides the ability to run off-the-shelf applications on any hardware running Open Desktop with a minimum of configuration requirements.

In the workstation market, several competing GUIs have been developed and had brief flurries of popularity. The manufacturer with the largest number of workstations in the market, Sun Microsystems, produced a GUI that again seems to be becoming a de facto standard: The Open Look Graphical User Interface. Open Look can be ported to other hardware, allowing applications to be moved between platforms. Open Look is also used as the interface to AT&T's UNIX.

Minicomputer and mainframe GUIs are rare, because few large computer systems can dedicate the system resources needed to support GUIs for all their stations. The need for high resolution consoles and mice also makes the use of a GUI impractical in many large installations. For these types of offices, it is more common to find a few terminals that support a graphics interface, with the rest of the terminals supporting the standard UNIX interface.

The Evolution of UNIX

The future of UNIX is bright. By coming to a set of standards that provides a single description for all future UNIX versions, the industry will solve application portability problems.

Despite its age, UNIX remains a fast, powerful, and competitive operating system that is not at all limiting. As new developments occur within the industry, they will be adopted by UNIX and then incorporated into newer products. All the while, though, UNIX will continue to offer a powerful means of controlling multiuser systems.

Appendix A

UNIX Commands and Options

This appendix is a complete listing of all the UNIX commands and a brief descriptions of their functions. You will find the commands described fully and used in examples in the various chapters of this book; here they serve as a quick reference for the reader. Also, see Appendix B for a quick, one-stop alphabetical listing of commands and options.

Table A.1: UNIX Commands by Operation

General listing of commands

Command, Switch, or Option	Description
date	displays system date and time
export	sets a UNIX variable (like **TERM**)
passwd	changes your password
TERM	defines your terminal type
who	lists all users currently on the system
cat	concatenates a file (display or copy)
cd	changes directory
copy	copies files or directories
cp	copies files
l	directory list
lc	columnar directory list
more	displays a file screen by screen

Table A.1: UNIX Commands by Operation (Continued)

General listing of commands (continued)

Command, Switch, or Option	Description
mv	renames (move) a file
pwd	prints current (working) directory
rm	deletes a file
rmdir	removes a directory
who	lists who is currently on the system
cal	displays a calendar
calendar	checks date for triggered events
cmp	compares files
diff	displays the differences between files
egrep	string search
fgrep	string search
find	finds a file
grep	string search
ln	links several filenames to one file
l	directory list
lc	columnar directory list
ls	directory list
sort	arranges entries in a file in order
wc	counts words, lines and characters
who	shows users currently on the system

Print and background processing commands

at	delays the start of a process
atrm	removes a process sent by **at**
cancel	cancels a print request
kill	terminates a process
lp	sends a file to the printer
lpstat	gets printer and spooler status
pr	paginates a file
ps	lists processes executing

mail commands

a	creates an alias (distribution list)
~b	adds names to the blind carbon copy list

Table A.1: UNIX Commands by Operation (Continued)

mail commands (continued)

Command, Switch, or Option	Description
~c	adds names to the carbon copy list
d	deletes displayed or specified (with a numeric argument) messages
dp	deletes displayed message and displays the next one
e	invokes editor
h	scrolls headers forward or back
f	forwards mail to another user
F	forwards mail without shifting text to the right
l	prints a hard copy
mb	saves message in your personal mailbox
n	skips n pieces of mail (+/-)
p	displays (print) mail
q	quits with cleanup of mailbox
r	replys to mail
R	replys to multiple users
restart	restarts mail and check for new messages
s	saves to a file
top	displays first five lines of specified messages
u	undeletes (restores) deleted mail
v	invokes vi
x	quits with no cleanup of mailbox
?	displays help screen summary
=	displays current message number
!	invokes a shell command without leaving mail

ed commands

a	adds or appends text to the end of the file
c	changes lines
d	deletes text
e	reads text from another file (destroys buffer!)
f	displays or change current working filename
i	inserts lines before the current line
p	prints lines from the buffer
r	reads text from another file (doesn't destroy buffer!)
u	undoes last substitution command

Table A.1: UNIX Commands by Operation (Continued)

ed commands (continued)

Command, Switch, or Option	Description
w	writes the buffer to a file
q	quits the editor
=	displays current line number
+	displays next line
-	displays previous line
.	quits text mode and enter command mode

vi cursor movement commands

b	back one word
h	left one character
j	down one line
k	up one line
l	right one character
w	forward one word
0	beginning of current line
$	end of current line
G	goes to a specific line
H	top left corner of screen
L	lowest line on screen
Ctrl-U	scrolls up 1/2 screen
Ctrl-D	scrolls down 1/2 screen
Ctrl-F	scrolls down 1 screen
Ctrl-B	scrolls up 1 screen

vi delete commands

dd	deletes current line
dw	deletes from cursor to end of word
x	deletes character cursor is on
d$	deletes from cursor to end of line
D	deletes from cursor to end of line
d0	deletes from cursor to start of line

Table A.1: UNIX Commands by Operation (Continued)

chmod command options for "who" argument

Command, Switch, or Option	Description
a	All users (this is the default if nothing is specified)
g	All users in the same group as the owner
o	All users on the system (stands for "others")
u	Owner (or user) of the file or directory

copy command options

-a	asks the user for confirmation before copying
-l	uses links instead of copying when possible
-n	requires a new destination: do not overwrite
-o	retains original owner and group information
-m	changes modification date and time to copy time
-r	recursive directory copy
-ad	asks for confirmation of directory copy
-v	verbose: displays file names as copied

find command options

-a	time nfile was accessed in the last n days
-c	time nfile had its inode changed in the last n days
-exec cmd	execute 'cmd' if the search is successful
-group	name has group 'name'
-links x	file has x links
-mtime n	file was modified in the last n days
-name	file matches 'name'
-newer	file was modified more recently than 'file'
-perm	perms has permissions that match octal 'perms'
-print	print pathname
-size n	file is n blocks long
-size nc	file is n characters long
-type x	file has type 'x' (b,c,d,p or f)
-user	name has owner 'name'

grep command options

-c	shows a count of all matching lines
-i	ignores case during comparisons

Table A.1: UNIX Commands by Operation (Continued)

grep command options (continued)

Command, Switch, or Option	Description
-l	shows only the names of files with matches in them
-n	precedes each line with its line number in file
-s	suppresses error messages
-v	displays all lines that don't match
-x	displays only exact matches of the entire line (**fgrep** only)
-y	ignores case

list command options

-a	lists all files, including hidden files
-d	lists only directories
-l	produces a long list (like the l command)
-r	lists files in reverse alphabetical order
-t	lists files by date of last modification, from the most recent backwards. (Combined with the -r option, it lists from oldest to most recent.)
-F	marks all directories with a backslash, and executables files with an asterisk
-R	lists files and directories recursively

ps command options

-e	shows all processes
-d	shows all processes except process group leaders
-a	same as "d" but also ignores terminal processes
-f	generates a full listing
-l	generates a long listing
-t	shows a list of processes associated with a terminal
-u	shows a list of processes associated with a user
-g	shows a list of processes associated with a group

sort command options

-R	lists files and directories recursively
-b	ignores any leading blanks
-c	checks that the file is already sorted

Table A.1: UNIX Commands by Operation (Continued)

sort command options (continued)

Command, Switch, or Option	Description
-d	sorts in dictionary order
-f	ignores case
-i	ignores non-printing characters
-n	orders numerically
-r	reverses the comparison order
-o	sends output to a specified file
-u	unique occurrences: ignore duplications of entries

test command options

-r file	true if 'file' exists and is readable
-w file	true if 'file' exists and is writeable
-x file	true if 'file' exists and is executable
-f file	true if 'file' exists and is a regular file
-d file	true if 'file' exists and is a directory
-u file	true if 'file' exists and its user-ID bit is set
-g file	true if 'file' exists and its group-ID bit is set
-s file	true if 'file' exists and its size is not 0
-z s1	true if the length of string 's1' is zero
-n s1	true if the length of string 's1' is not zero
s1 = s2	true if strings 's1' and 's2' are identical
s1 != s2	true if strings 's1' and 's2' are not identical
s1	true if 's1' is not the null string

algebraic test statements

n1 -eq n2	true if integers 'n1' and 'n2' are equal
n1 -ne n2	true if integers 'n1' and 'n2' are not equal
n1 -gt n2	true if integer 'n1' is greater than 'n2'
n1 -ge n2	true if integer 'n1' is greater than or equal to 'n2'
n1 -lt n2	true if integer 'n1' is less than 'n2'
n1 -le n2	true if integer 'n1' is less than or equal to 'n2'

Switches for the tar command

r	writes to end of existing archive
x	extracts from the archive (recursive)

Table A.1: UNIX Commands by Operation (Continued)

Switches for the tar command (continued)

Command, Switch, or Option	Description
t	lists names of files in archives as they occur
u	files added if not modified or archived already
c	creates a new archive media

Modifiers for the tar command

0-7	specifies the drive to be archived
A	suppresses absolute filenames
b	provides a blocking factor of 1-20 (tape only)
e	prevents splitting files across volumes
f	gives the archive media device name
F	gives the name of a file for tar arguments
k	gives size of archive volume in kilobytes
l	displays error messages if links unresolved
m	does not restore modification times
n	indicates the archive is not a tape
p	extracts files with their original permissions
v	verbose output (lists files on the console)

Commands for peripherals

cancel	cancels a printer request
disable	deactivates a port
enable	activates a port
lp	routes to the printer
lp move	moves a printer request to another printer
lpsched	starts the print spooler
lpshut	stops the print spooler
lpstat	displays print and scheduler status information
reject	prevents requests from going to specified printer

Shell predefined variables

HOME	defines your login directory
IFS	internal field separator character
MAIL	pathname for your mail box
PATH	directory search list for commands

Table A.1: UNIX Commands by Operation (Continued)

Shell predefined variables (continued)

Command, Switch, or Option	Description
PSI	primary prompt string
PS2	secondary prompt string

Appendix B

Alphabetical Listing of Commands

Table B.1 is provided for quick reference. It is a complete alphabetical listing of all the UNIX commands and options explained in this book. Some of the options for different commands are physically the same, so a distinction has been made—you will see the appropriate command listed next to the option.

Table B.1: Alphabetical Listing of Commands (

A

Command or Option	Description
A	supresses absolute filenames
a (chmod)	all users (this is the default if nothing is specified)
a (ed)	adds or appends text to the end of file
a (mail)	creates an alias (distribution list)
at	delasy the start of a process
-a (copy)	asks the user for confirmation before copying
-a (find)	time nfile was accessed in the last n days
-a (list)	list all files, including hidden files
-a (ps)	same as "d" but also ignores terminal processes
-ad	asks for confirmation of directory copy

B

b (modifiers for tar)	provides a blocking factor of 1-20 (tape only)
b (vi)	moves back one word

Table B.1: Alphabetical Listing of Commands (Continued)

B (continued)

Command or Option	Description
-b (sort)	ignores any leading blanks
~b	adds names to the blind carbon copy list

C

Command or Option	Description
c (ed)	changes lines
c (switches for tar)	creates a new archive media
cal	displays a calendar
calendar	checks date for triggered events
cancel (peripheral)	cancels a printer request
cancel (print and background)	cancels a print request
cat	concatenates a file (display or copy)
cd	changes directory
cmp	compares files
copy	copies files or directories
cp	copies files
Ctrl-B	scrolls up 1 screen
Ctrl-D	scrolls down 1/2 screen
Ctrl-F	scrolls down 1 screen
Ctrl-U	scrolls up 1/2 screen
-c (grep)	shows a count of all matching lines
-c (find)	time nfile had its inode changed in the last n days
-c (sort)	checks that the file is already sorted
~c	adds names to the carbon copy list

D

Command or Option	Description
D	deletes from cursor to end of line
d (ed)	deletes text
d (mail)	deletes displayed or specified (with a numeric argument) messages
date	displays system date and time
dd (vi)	deletes current line
diff	displays the differences between files
disable	deactivates a port
dp	deletes dsiplayed message and displays the next one

Table B.1: Alphabetical Listing of Commands (Continued)

D (continued)

Command or Option	Description
dw	deletes from cursor to end of word
d0	deletes from cursor to start of line
d$	deletes from cursor to end of line
-d file	true if 'file' exists and is a directory
-d (list)	lists only directories
-d (ps)	shows all processes except process group leaders
-d (sort)	sorts in dictionary order

E

Command or Option	Description
e (ed)	reads text from another file (destroys buffer!)
e (mail)	invokes editor
e (modifiers for tar)	prevents splitting files across volumes
egrep	string search
enables	activates a port
export	sets a UNIX variable (like TERM)
-e (ps)	shows all processes
-exec cmd	executes 'cmd" if the search is successful

F

Command or Option	Description
F (mail)	forwards mail without shifting text to the right
F (modifiers for tar)	gives the name of a file for tar arguments
f (ed)	displays or changes current working filename
f (mail)	forwards mail to another user
f (modifiers for tar)	gives the archive media device name
f grep	string search
find	finds a file
-F (list)	marks all directories with a backslash, and executable files with an asterisk
-f files	true if 'file' exists and is a reguular file
-f (ps)	generates a full listing
-f (sort)	ignores case

Table B.1: Alphabetical Listing of Commands (Continued)

G

Command or Option	Description
G	goes to a specific line
g (chmod)	All users in the same group as the owner
grep	string search
-g (ps)	shows a list of processes associated with a group
-g file	true if 'file' exists and its group-ID bit is set
-group	name has group 'name'

H

H	top left corner of screen
h (mail)	scrolls headers forward or back
h (vi)	moves left one character
HOME	defines your login directory

I

i	inserts lines before the current line
IFS	internal field separator character
-i (grep)	ignores case during comparisons
-i (sort)	ignores non-printing characters

J

j	moves down one line

K

k (modifiers for tar)	gives size of archive volume in kilobytes
K (vi)	moves up one line
kill	terminates a process

L

L	lowest line on screen
l (general)	directory list
l (mail)	prints a hard copy
l (modifiers for tar)	displays error messages if links unresolved
l (vi)	moves right one character

Table B.1: Alphabetical Listing of Commands (Continued)

L (continued)

Command or Option	Description
lc	columnar directory list
ln	links several filenames to one file
lp (peripherals)	route to the printer
lp (print and background)	sends a file to the printer
lp move	moves a printer request to antoher printer
lpsched	starts the print spooler
lpshut	stops the print spooler
lpstat (peripherals)	displays print and scheduler status information
lpstat (print and background)	gets printer and spooler status
ls	directory list
-l (copy)	uses links instead of copying when possible
-l (grep)	shows only the name of files with matches in them
-l (list)	produces a long list (like the l command)
-l (ps)	generates a long listing
-links x	file has x links

M

Command or Option	Description
m (modifiers for tar)	does not restore modification times
MAIL	pathname for your mailbox
mb	saves message in your personal mailbox
more	displays a file screen by screen
mv	renames (move) a file
-m (copy)	changes modification date and time to copy time
-mtime n	file was modified in the last n days

N

Command or Option	Description
n (mail)	skip n pieces of mail (=/-)
n (modifiers for tar)	indicates the archive is not a tape
n1 -eq n2	true if intergers 'n1' and 'n2' are equal
n1 -ge n2	true if interger 'n1' is greater than or equal to 'n2"
n1 -gt n2	true if interger 'n1' is greater than 'n2'
n1 -le n2	true if interger 'n1' is less than or equal to 'n2'
n1 -lt 2n	true if interger 'n1' is less than 'n2'
n1 -ne n2	true if intergers 'n1' and 'n2' are not equal

Table B.1: Alphabetical Listing of Commands (Continued)

N (continued)

Command or Option	Description
-n (copy)	requires a new destination: do not overwrite
-n (grep)	precedes each line with its line number in file
-n (sort)	orders numerically
-n s1	true if the length of string 's1' is not zero
-name	file matches 'name'
newer	file was modified more recently than 'file'

O

o	All users on the system (stands for "others")
-o (copy)	retains original owner and group information
-o (sort)	sends output to a specified file

P

p (ed)	prints lines from the buffer
p (mail)	displays (prints) mail
p (modifiers for tar)	extracts files with their original permissions
passwd	changes your password
PATH	directory search list for commands
pr	paginates a file
ps	lists processes executing
PS1	primary prompt string
PS2	secondary prompt string
pwd	prints current (working) directory
-perm	perms has permissions that match octal 'perms'
-print	prints pathname

Q

q (ed)	quits the editor
q (mail)	quits with cleanup of mailbox

R

R	replies to multiple users
r (ed)	reads text from another file (doesn't destroy buffer!)

Table B.1: Alphabetical Listing of Commands (Continued)

R (continued)

Command or Option	Description
r (mail)	replies to mail
r (switches for tar)	writes to end of existing archive
reject	prevents requests from going to a specified printer
restart	restarts mail and checks for new messages
rm	deletes a file
rmdir	removes a directory
-R (list)	lists files and directories
-R (sort)	lists files and directories recursively
-r (copy)	recursive directory copy
-r (list)	lists files in reverse alphabetical order
-r (sort)	reverses the comparison order
-r file	true if 'file' exists and is readable

S

Command or Option	Description
s (mail)	saves to a file
sort	arranges entries in a file in order
s1	true if 's2' is not the null string
s1 = s2	true if strings strings 's1' and 's2' are identical
s1! = s2	true if strings 's1' and 's2' are not identical
-s	suppresses error messages
-s file	true if 'file' exists and its size is not 0
-size n	file is n blocks long
-size nc	file is n characters long

T

Command or Option	Description
t (switches for tar)	lists names of files in archives as they occur
top	displays first five lines of specified messages
-t (list)	lists files by date of last modification, from the most recent backwards. (combined with the -r option, it lists from oldest to most recent.)
-t (ps)	shows a list of processes associated with a terminal
-type x	file has type 'x' (b,c,d,p,or f)

Table B.1: Alphabetical Listing of Commands (Continued)

u

Command or Option	Description
u (chmod)	Owner (or user) of the file or directory
u (ed)	undoes last substitution command
u (mail)	undeletes (restores) deleted mail
u (switches for tar)	files added if not modified or archived already
-u file	true if 'file' exists and its user-ID bit is set
-u (ps)	shows a list of processes assocated with a user
-u (sort)	unique occurences: ignore duplications of entries
-user	name has owner 'name'

v

v	invokes vi
v (modifier for tar)	verbose output (lists files on the console)
-v (copy)	verbose: displays file names as copied
-v (grep)	displays all lines that don't match

w

w (ed)	writes the buffer to a file
w (vi)	moves forward one word
wc	counts words, lines, and characters
who	lists all users currently on the system
-w file	true if 'file' exists and is writeable

x

x (mail)	quits with no cleanup of mailbox
x (switches for tar)	extract from the archive (recursive)
x (vi)	deletes character cursor is on
-x file	true if 'file' exists and is executable
-x (grep)	displays only exact matches of the entire line (**fgrep** only)

y

-y (grep)	ignores case

Table B.1: Alphabetical Listing of Commands (Continued)

Z

Command or Option	Description
-z s1	true if the length of string 's1' is zero

Miscellaneous

(mail)

?	displays help screen summary
=	displays current message number
!	invokes a shell command without leaving mail

(ed)

=	displays current line number
+	displays next line
-	displays previous line
.	quits text mode and enters command mode

(vi)

0	moves to beginning of current line
$	moves to end of current line

Index

A

Absolute mode, chmod command, 181, 183
Accept command, 212
Account, 12
Acctcom command, 196-197
Accton command, 195-196
a command, 75
Alias command, 70
Aliasing, 124-125
Ampersand, 57
Application software, 3
ASCII file, 106
Asterisk, 102
    wildcard, 29
At command
    at-1 command, 56
    at-r command, 56
    delaying process, 55
    format for, 55
Atime option, find command, 99
At program, 169-170

B

~b, 63
Background processing, 56-57
    operation of, 57
Backslashes, use with meta characters, 122-123
Backups
    backup account, 191-192
    importance of, 185
    log for, 190-191
    media for, 187-188
    schedule for, 188-189
    tar program, 192-195

Bell Telephone Laboratories, 5, 6
Berkeley Software Distribution
    UNIX, 6
Bin directory, 39
Body, of mail, 62
Booting system, 151-152
Bourne shell, 116, 124-125
Break command, 146-147
Buffer, vi editor, 92-94

C

~c, 63
Calendar, 111-112, 168
    date-based reminders, 112
Cal program, 111-112
Cancel command, printing, 54-55
Carbon copies, of mail, 62, 63, 64
Case of letters, caution about, 22, 26
Case statement, 142-144
Cat command, 52, 123, 124
    display of files, 30-31
c command, 80
/c command, list of files, 28-29
Cd command, moving through directories, 42-43
Central processing unit, 2
Characters, counting, 106
Chgrp command, 184

Child process, 172
Chmod command, 123, 181-184
    absolute mode, 181, 183
    symbolic mode, 181-182
    for who argument, 182
    wildcards, 183
Chown command, 164, 184
cmp command, comparing files, 103-104
co command, 92
Command mode, 64, 74
    vi editor, 85, 86
Comparing files
    cmp command, 103-104
    diff command, 104-105
Compose escape, of mail, 63
Compose mode, of mail, 63, 65
Computers
    components of, 2-3
    damage, sources of, 185-187
Conditional looping, 144
Continue command, 146-147
Copy command, 166-167
Copying files
    copy command, 166-167
    cp command, 35, 166-167
    from directories, 46-47
Copying lines, vi editor, 92-93
Core, 98

Core dump, 156
Counting, lines/words/characters, 106
Cp command, 166-167
    copying files, 35
Crash, system crash, 185-187
Cron program, 156, 157, 167-169
Crontab program, 167-168
C Shell, 19, 116, 124, 125
Ctrl-B, 95
Ctrl-D, 15, 64, 65, 95
Ctrl-F, 95
Ctrl-Q, 31
Ctrl-S, 31
Ctrl-U, 95
Current line, vi editor, 85

D

Damaged files, fsck program, 152
Dash character, 119
Date, at program, 169
Date command, 22
Day, in at command, 56
d command, 68-69, 79, 89
dd command, 89
Default printer, 51
Deleting files, rm command, 33-35
Deleting lines, ed editor, 79
Deleting text, vi editor, 89-90

Del key, 32
Dev directory, 39, 201
Device files, 199-201
    block mode device, 200
    character mode device, 200
    directory of, 201
    mnemonic code to identify devices, 200-201
    numbers assigned to devices, 201
df command, 157-158
diff command
    comparing files, 104-105
    options in, 105
Digital Equipment VT-100 terminal, 16
Directories
    bin directory, 39
    copying files from, 46-47
    creating directories, 43-45
    dev directory, 39
    etc directory, 39
    home directory, 40-42
    moving through, 42-43
    name of, 40
    removing directories, 45-46
    renaming directories, 46
    root directory, 39
    tree analogy, 39, 40
    usr directory, 40

Disable command, 212
Disk swapping, 155
Display of files
    cat command, 30-31
    more command, 32-33
Document creation, vi editor, 85-86
Do later program, 56
Dollar sign, 128, 134
dp command, 69
du command, 158
dw command, 89

E

Echo commands, 143, 144
e command, 65, 77
Ed editor, 74-84
    changing lines, 80
    deleting lines, 79
    entering text, 75-76
    inserting lines, 79
    invoking editor, 74-75
    last line of text, 78
    math functions, 78
    moving from line to line, 78-79
    moving lines, 80
    reading in existing file, 76-77
    replacing text, 82-84
    searching for text, 80-81

Editors
    command mode, 74
    ed editor, 74-84
    line editors, 74
    screen editors, 74
    text mode, 74
    vi editor, 85-94
Egrep command, 110-111
Emulation modes, 18
Enable command, 212
Equal, = command, 67
Errors, memory area written to core, 98
Etc directory, 39
Etc/ group, 159-160
/etc/passwd file, 163
/etc/rc file, 156, 195-196
Eval statement, 165
Exec command, 166
Exit
    Exit command, 147
    exiting programs, 32-33
    logging out, 15
Export command, 17, 133, 135-136, 165

F

f command, 69, 70, 77

Fgrep command, 110-111
Files
   comparing files
     cmp command, 103-104
     diff command, 104-105
   copying files, cp command, 35
   counting lines/words/characters in, 106
   deleting files, rm command, 33-35
   display of files
     cat command, 30-31
     more program, 32-33
   finding file, 97-99
   linking files, 99-101
   list of files
     /c command, 28-29
     ls command, 101-102
     l command, 26
     printing list, 102-103
     wildcard characters, 29-30
   naming files, 25-26
   nature of, 25
   permissions, 36-37
   piping, 38
   redirection, 37-38
   renaming files, mv command, 35
   searching for patterns, 109-111
   sorting file, 106-108

File system, nature of, 7
Find command, 156, 164
Finding file, 97-99
   find command, 97-99
     atime option, 99
     group option, 99
     mtime option, 99
     user option, 99
     recursive search, 98
Firmware, nature of, 2
Flow control commands. *See* Program flow
Foreground process, 57
Fork, 117
Forked process, 172
Forking process, 172
For loop, 145-146
Fsck program, 152

G

g command, 83-84, 87
Graphical user interfaces (GUI)
   advantages of, 217-218
   development of, 218-220
   expansion of, 221-222
   windows, 216-217
   X Windows, 220-221
  character, 120-121
   start, 122

Grep command, 109-111
Group option, find command, 99
Grpcheck program, 160

H

Haltsys command, 154
Hard disk
    free space
        checking free space, 157-158
        maintaining, 155-157
        thrashing, 155
Hardware, nature of, 2
Header, of mail, 62, 64
History, 124
HOME, 41, 133
Home directory, 13, 40-42

I

i command, 79
ID
    printing and, 54
    user groups and, 160, 161, 163
Idle out command, 177
Idleout kills command, 177
If command, 138-142
    of Bourne shell, 138
    if/else, 140-142
    if/then/else, 138-140
    nesting of, 140-142
IFS, 133
I (interactive) option, 34
in command, linking files, 99-101
Inserting lines, ed editor, 79
Insert mode, vi editor, 85
Iteration. *See* Looping

J

Job control, 125

K

Kernel, 199-200
    nature of, 7
Kernighan, Brian, 5
Kill command, 172-173
    stop background processing, 58
Korn shell, 116, 125-126

L

character, 120-121
Line editors, 74
Lines, counting, 106
Linking files, 99-101
    finding information on linked files, 100

List of files
    /c command, 28-29
    ls command, 101-102
    1 command, 26
    printing list, 102-103
    wildcard characters, 29-30
Log, backup log, 190-191
Log files, 157
Logging in, 12-15
    home directory, 13
    login, 12-14
    password, 13-14
    shell prompt characters, 14-15
    user names, 12-13
Logging out, 15-18
    Ctrl-D, 15
    exit, 15
    logout, 15
Login, 12-14
.login, 165-166
Logons, 12
Logout, 15
Looping
    breaking a loop, 146-147
    conditional looping, 144
    continuing a loop, 146-147
    for loop, 145-146
    while loop, 144-146
Lp command
    m option, 52
    print spooler, 50-51
    w option, 51
lpmove command, 211
lpshut command, 210
lpstat command, 210, 211, 212
    printer status information, 52-54
Lpstat-t command, 54
ls command, options in, 101-102

M

MAIL, 133
    carbon copies, 62, 63, 64
    components of mail, 62
    compose escape, 63
    compose mode, 63, 65
    customizing settings for, 71
    deleting mail, 68-69
    example of use, 63-64
    forwarding mail message, 69-70
    mailing lists, 70-71
    reading mail, 65-67
    replying to mail message, 69
    saving mail, 67-68
    sending mail, 65
    system mailbox, 62
    undeleting mail, 69
    user mailbox, 62
    versions of, 61-62
.mailre file, 71

Mandatory file locking permission, 182
Math functions, ed editor, 78
mb command, 67
m command, 80
Mean time between failure, 187
Memory, computer, 2
Meta characters, 122-123
    of UNIX, 109
    use as literal character, 122-123
mkdev lp command, 209
Mkdir command, creating directories, 43-45
Mkuser command, 160-162
Modems, 207
More command, 139, 142
    display of files, 32-33
    piping, 38
More program, 80
    exiting program, 32-33
    tasks performed by, 32-33
Motd (message of the day), 14
Moving lines, ed editor, 80
Moving text, vi editor, 93-94
Mtime option, find command, 99
Multics, 5
Multitasking, meaning of, 3
Multiuser system, 3
Mv command, renaming files, 35

N

Naming files, 25-26
    renaming files, 35
n command, 66
Nesting, if/else command, 140-142
Newgrp program, 160
Null device, 57

O

1 command
    file permissions, 36
    list of files, 26
1s-1 command, list of files, 27
Open Desktop, 221-222
Operating modes
    normal, 152
    system maintenance mode, 152-153, 154-155
Operating system, 3
    nature of, 2-3
Overwriting text, 88

P

Pagination of files, 52
Parent process, 172
Passwd command, 164, 177
Passwords, 176-178

case conventions and, 14
changing user passwords,
    29021, 177-178
  passwd command, 20, 177
  pwadmin command, 177-178
choosing password, 21, 176
logging in, 13-14
password aging, 177-178
supervisor password, 176
unmatched passwords, 21
user groups and, 161-162, 163-164
PATH, 117-119, 133
  system variables, 117
    PS1, 118-119
    PS2, 118
  viewing path, 117
p command, 66, 75-76, 82
Periods, directory notation, 43
Peripherals
  device files, 199-201
  modems, 207
  printers, 207-213
  terminals, 201-207
Permissions
  changing of
    chgrp command, 184
    chmod command, 181-184
    chown command, 184
  default directory permissions, 180
  default permission mask, 180-181
  display of, 179
  for file or directory, 182
  listing of, 36
  mandatory file locking permission, 182
  read and write permissions, 182-183
  types of, 36-37
  user/group/other, 179
  valid file types, 179
Piping, 38, 120-121
  characters for, 37
  more command, 38
  pipe symbols, 120-121
  sorting and, 108
Positional variables, 129-130
POSIX, standard, 216
Power conditioners, 187
Pr command, pagination of files, 52
Predefined variables, 133-134
  listing of, 133
Primitives, 9
Printers, 207-213
  background process, 49
  canceling print request, 54-55

connecting printer, 208-209
default printer, 51
parallel printers, 52
print spooler, 50, 51
redirecting file to, 52
sending file to, 50-52
serial printers, 52
status information about, 52-54
Printing
directory listings, 102-103
ID number, 54
Print spooler, 102-103, 209-213
control of, 211-213
request ID, 210
startup/shutdown of, 210
Process
automation of
cron program, 167-169
at program, 169-170
background processing, 56-57
child process, 172
delaying start of, 55-56
forked process, 172
forking process, 172
killing process, 57-58, 172-173
parent process, 172
process ID, 55
Process accounting
accessing information, 196-197
nature of, 195
starting of, 195-196
stopping of, 196
Processor status, 170-173
headers/meanings in, 171
options in, 170-171
process flags, 172
process states, 172
.profile, 164-165
.profile file, 135-136
Program, computer, 3
Program flow, 136-147
break command, 146-147
case statement, 142-144
continue command, 146-147
exit command, 147
if command, 138-142
for loop, 145-146
test command, 137-138
while loop, 144-146
PS1, 133
PS2, 133
Ps command, 170-172
lists process executing, 58
options in, 170-171
to terminate process, 171
Pwadmin command, 177-178
Pwcheck command, 164

Q

q command, 64, 66, 76
Q (quit), 32
Question mark, wildcard, 29
Qume QUT 101+ terminal, 16
Quotation marks, 132

R

r command, 69, 77
Read statement, 143
Read and write permissions, 182-183
Redirection, 37-38
    characters for, 37
    sending file to printer, 52
    sorting and, 108
Redirect symbol, 26, 31, 37
Reject command, 212
Renaming files, mv command, 35
Repeat command, 87-88
Replacing text
    ed editor, 82-83
    vi editor, 91-92
Restart command, 68
Return code, 104
Ritchie, Dennis, 5-6
Rm command
    deleting files, 33-35
    wildcard characters, 33-34

Rmdir command, removing directories, 45-46
Rmuser, 162-163
Root directory, 39

S

Santa Cruz Operation, 6
Saving files, 86-87
s command, 68, 82
Screen display, more program, 32
Screen editors, 74
Scrolling, stopping, 31
Searching for patterns, 109-111
    egrep command, 110-111
    fgrep command, 110-111
    grep command, 109-111
Searching for text
    backward searches, 81, 91
    ed editor, 80-81
    more program, 80
    vi editor, 90-91
Security
    passwords, 176-178
    permissions, 179-185
    physical security, 175-176
Semicolons, between commands, 22
Separator, slash character, 39
Set command, 117, 130
Shell, 18-19

aliasing, 124-125
Bourne shell, 19, 116, 124-125
  creating program, 123-124
C shell, 116, 124, 125
  fork, 117
  history, 124
  job control, 125
Korn shell, 116, 125-126
nature of, 7, 18-19
parsing, 136
program flow, 136-147
  break command, 146-147
  case statement, 142-144
  continue command, 146-147
  exit command, 147
  if command, 138-142
  for loop, 145-146
  test command, 137-138
  while loop, 144-146
shell scripts, 127
Shell escape, 90
Shell prompt character, 19, 21
  logging in, 14-15
Shell scripts, 127
Shell variables, 128-136
  positional variables, 129-130
  predefined variables, 133-134
  .profile file, 135-136
  user-defined variables, 130-133
  value of, 128-129

Shift command, 130
Shutdown command, 153-154
Shutdown su command, 154-155
Slash character, 33, 39
Software
  application software, 3
  nature of, 2
  operating system, 3
Sorting file, 106-108
  saving sorted file, 107
  sort command, 106-107
    options in, 107-108
    redirection/piping and, 108
Square brackets, with wildcards, 119-120
Standards, UNIX and, 215-216
Status line, vi editor, 86
Strings
  nature of, 128
  searching for patterns
    egrep command, 110-111
    fgrep command, 110-111
    grep command, 109-111
Subdirectories, PATH, 117-119
Symbolic mode, chmod command, 181-182
Sync command, 154
System administrator
  automation of process, 167-170
  booting system, 151-152

copying files, 166-167
disk space
  checking free space, 157-158
  freeing disk space, 155-157
.login, 165-166
maintenance of file systems, 155
processor status, 170-173
.profile, 165-166
shutdown of system, 153-154
superuser account, 150-151
system maintenance mode, 152-153, 154-155
tasks of, 149-150
user accounts, maintenance of, 158
user groups, 159-164
System mailbox, 62
System maintenance mode, 152-153, 154-155
  accessing system in, 153
  moving to, without rebooting, 154-155
System variables, 117
  PS1, 118-119
  PS2, 118

T

Tape archive program, tar, 192-195
Tar program
  backups, 192-195
  blocking factor, 194
  floppy disks, 194-195
  modifiers, 193
  switches, 192, 193
Task, 4
TERM command, 17
Terminals, 201-207
  adding terminal, 204-206
  changing terminal type, 17
  Digital Equipment VT-100 terminal, 16
  emulation modes, 18
  "/etc/gettydefs file, 203-204, 205
  "/etc/termcap file, 204, 205
  "/etc/ttys file, 201-202, 205
  "/etc/ttytype file, 203, 205
  getty on system, 203, 206
  hard-wired terminal, 12
  identification of, 16-17
  Qume QUT 101+ terminal, 16
  troubleshooting, 206-207
  Wyse 60 terminal, 16
Termname, 17
Test command, 137-138, 139
  algebraic test statements, 138
  options in, 137-138
Text mode, 74
Thompson, Ken, 5-6
Thrashing, 155

Tilde, 63
  vi editor, 85
Time
  in at command, 55
  at program, 169
Tools, nature of, 7
Top command, 67

U

u command, 69, 84, 88, 92
Underscore character, 64
UNIX
  advantages of, 7-9
  booting system, 151-152
  commands, listing of, 225-232
  development of, 5-7
  graphical user interfaces (GUI), 216-222
  identification of terminal, 16-18
  logging in, 12-15
  logging out, 15-16
  operating modes, 152-153
  parts of, 7
    file system, 7
    kernel, 7
    shell, 7
    tools, 7
  password, 20-21
  shell, 18-19
  shutdown of system, 153-154
  standards, 215-216
  terminals and, 11-12
  use on microcomputers, 6-7
  versions of, 215
  See also individual topics.
UNIX commands, vi editor and, 90
Unmask command, 165, 180-181
User-defined variables, 130-133
User groups, 159-164
  adding new group, 159-162
  changing user, 163-164
  etc/ group, 159-160
  nature of, 159
  removing user, 162-163
User mailbox, 62
User names, logging in, 12-13
User option, find command, 99
/usr/adm/pacct file, 196
Usr directory, 40

V

Value, of variable, 128-129, 132, 134
Variables
  nature of, 128
  See also Shell variables.
v command, 65, 83-84
Vertical bar symbol, 38
Vi editor, 85-94

buffer, 92-94
command mode, 85, 86
copying lines, 92-93
creating document, 85-86
current line, 85
deleting text, 89-90
exiting, 86
insert mode, 85
moving around screen, 87
moving text, 93-94
overwriting text, 88
repeating insert/delete command, 88
replace mode, 89
replacing text, 89, 91-92
saving files, 86-87
searching for text, 90-91
status line, 86
undo, 88
UNIX commands while working, 90

W

wc command, 106, 121, 123
w command, 76

While loop, 144-146
Who command, 19-20, 26, 27, 121, 123
    options, 20
Wildcard characters
    asterisk, 29
    chmod command, 183
    deleting files, 33-34
    list of files, 29-30
    matching characters in file name, 29
    question mark, 29
    square brackets, use of, 119-120
    use of two together, 30
Words, counting, 106, 119
Wyse 60 terminal, 16

X

XENIX, 6
X Windows, 220-221

Y

Yanking, copying lines, 92-93

compress ☐ -vd ☐ filename → to compress

compress ☐ -d ☐ filename → un-compress